RESEARCH
METHODOLOGY

RESEARCH METHODOLOGY

A HANDBOOK FOR BEGINNERS

PAGADALA SUGANDA DEVI

Notion Press

Old No. 38, New No. 6
McNichols Road, Chetpet
Chennai - 600 031

First Published by Notion Press 2017
Copyright © Pagadala Suganda Devi 2017
All Rights Reserved.

ISBN 978-1-947752-83-2

This book has been published with all reasonable efforts taken to make the material error-free after the consent of the author. No part of this book shall be used, reproduced in any manner whatsoever without written permission from the author, except in the case of brief quotations embodied in critical articles and reviews.

The Author of this book is solely responsible and liable for its content including but not limited to the views, representations, descriptions, statements, information, opinions and references ["Content"]. The Content of this book shall not constitute or be construed or deemed to reflect the opinion or expression of the Publisher or Editor. Neither the Publisher nor Editor endorse or approve the Content of this book or guarantee the reliability, accuracy or completeness of the Content published herein and do not make any representations or warranties of any kind, express or implied, including but not limited to the implied warranties of merchantability, fitness for a particular purpose. The Publisher and Editor shall not be liable whatsoever for any errors, omissions, whether such errors or omissions result from negligence, accident, or any other cause or claims for loss or damages of any kind, including without limitation, indirect or consequential loss or damage arising out of use, inability to use, or about the reliability, accuracy or sufficiency of the information contained in this book.

Contents

About the Author   vii

Preface   ix

Chapter 1: Basic Concepts of Research   1

Chapter 2: Nature of Research   14

Chapter 3: Identifying Research Problem   34

Chapter 4: Literature review – Need, Objectives and Reporting   46

Chapter 5: Research Design   52

Chapter 6: Hypothesis Designing   63

Chapter 7: Determining the Objects of Analysis   77

Chapter 8: Data Collection   90

Chapter 9: Data Analysis   109

Chapter 10: Testing of Hypothesis   132

Chapter 11: Report Writing   155

References   175

About the Author

Pagadala Sugandha Devi is Assistant Professor, in Department of Accounting & Finance, at Arsi University, Ethiopia. She is also a research scholar at Hyderabad Business School (HBS), Gitam University, Hyderabad campus. She has about 20 years of teaching experience (10 years in India and about 10 years in Ethiopia) in various areas of finance, with a passion for research. She has published 1 text book, 9 study notes and 8 research based articles in reputed journals so far.

In her academic carrier spanning over 20 years, she has advised more than 100 masters students in their thesis and examined equal number as internal and external examiner. She also worked as a guest faculty member with Jawaharlal Nehru Technological University (JNTU) Hyderabad. Currently she teaches 'Research Methodology' course at Addis Ababa Science & Technology University (AASTU) as a part time teacher.

Preface

Academic research has become a necessity for many and passion for a few. Like everyone else in my field, I started research for academic interests. However, I can now feel that I have developed a passion for it. Most of the academic research done nowadays is superficial with almost no knowledge of research methodology. Research is mostly done for academic promotions, fund utilization or for getting a degree. Very few are successful in adding to the available content of knowledge. In my initial pursuits of conducting research, I always felt that most of the available text books are not user friendly for beginners. This led to a research on length and depth of many renowned text books in 'Research Methodology' and finally what I gathered as a note for myself is presented as a 'Hand book for Beginners.'

I request all my readers to extend their valuable suggestions so that this handbook could be made more useful to students who are venturing into research as 'beginners.'

Chapter 1

Basic Concepts of Research

Technology has brought about many changes in contemporary business world. Some of these changes are welcome while other have resulted in a number of new generation problems. Research is identified as a tool to find solutions to the various business problems. Though research is not a solution by itself, it will however equip managers with new insights so that they find plausible solutions to frequent mushrooming problems.

Meaning of Research

Research is a process of seeking answers to certain questions which have not been answered so far. This is a basic definition of 'Research.' However a point to ponder is "Is the answer of a question in an examination is also research?" The answer is a definite 'NO,' because the answers of these questions are available. They are answered by someone else somewhere else. They are openly available in text-books, class-notes etc. Research answers only those questions of which the answers are not available in literature i.e., in human knowledge. Thus, we can say research seeks the answer only of those questions of which the answers can be given on the basis of available facilities.

Actually research is simply the process of arriving at a dependable solution to a problem through planned and systematic collection, analysis and interpretation of data. Research is the most important process for advancing knowledge for promoting progress and to enable man to relate more effectively to his environment to accomplish his purpose and to resolve his conflicts. Research is devoted to find the conditions under which a certain phenomenon occurs and the conditions under which it does not occur in what might appear to be similar circumstances.

The term 'Research' consists of two words:

Research = Re + Search

'Re' means again and again and 'Search' means to find out something.

Therefore, research means to observe the phenomena again and again from different dimensions. Research is oriented towards the discovery of relationship that exists among phenomena of the world in which we live. The fundamental assumption is that invariant relationship exists between certain antecedents and certain consequents so that under a specific set of conditions a certain consequents can be expected to follow the introduction of a given antecedent.

Definitions of Research

Research is perceived differently by different authors. There are a variety of definitions in literature. Some of those definitions are discussed in the following sections.

According to the Encyclopedia of Social Sciences. Mac-Milan

Research refers to a critical and exhaustive investigation of experimentation having as its aim the revision of accepted conclusions in the light of new discovered facts.

According to Rusk

"Research is a point of view, an attitude of inquiry or a frame of mind. It asks questions which have hitherto not been asked, and it seeks to answer them by following a fairly definite procedure. It is not a mere theorising, but rather an attempt to elicit facts and to face them once they have been assembled. Research is likewise not an attempt to bolster up pre-conceived opinions, and it implies a readiness to accept the conclusions to which an inquiry leads, no matter how unwelcome they may prove. When successful, research adds to the scientific knowledge of the subject.

According to George J. Mouly

He defines research as, "The systematic and scholarly application of the scientific method interpreted in its broader sense, to the solution of social studies problems; conversely, any systematic study designed to promote the development of social studies as a science can be considered research."

According to Francis G. Cornell

"To be sure the best research is that which is reliable verifiable and exhaustive, so that it provides information in which we have confidence. The main point here is that research is, literally speaking, a kind of human behavior, an activity in which people engage. By this definition all intelligent human behavior involves some research."

According to C.C. Crawford

He writes that "Research is simply a systematic and refined technique of thinking, employing specialized tools, instruments, and procedures in order to obtain a more adequate solution of a problem than would be possible under ordinary means. It starts with a problem, collects data or facts, analysis these critically and reaches decisions based on the actual evidence. It evolves original work instead of mere exercise of personal. It evolves from a genuine desire to know rather than a desire to prove something.

According to C. Francies Rummel

"Research is an endeavour to discover, develop and verify knowledge. It is an intellectual process that has developed over hundreds of years, ever changing in purpose and form and always searching for truth."

P.M. Cook has given a very comprehensive and functional definition of the term research

"Research is an honest exhaustive, intelligent searching for facts and their meanings or implications with reference to a given problem. The product or findings of a given piece of research should be an authentic, verifiable and contribution to knowledge in the field studied."

He has emphasized the following characteristics of research in his definition:

1. It is an honest and exhaustive process.
2. The facts are studied with understanding.

3. The facts are discovered in the light of problem. Research is problem-centered.
4. The findings are valid and verifiable.
5. Research work should contribute new knowledge in that field.

General Characteristics of Research

The following characteristics may be gathered from the definitions of 'Research'

1. It gathers new knowledge or data from primary or first-hand sources.
2. It places emphasis upon the discovery of general principles.
3. It is an exact systematic and accurate investigation.
4. It uses certain valid data gathering devices.
5. It is logical and objective.
6. The researcher resists the temptation to seek only the data that support his hypotheses.
7. The researcher eliminates personal feelings and preferences.
8. It endeavors to organize data in quantitative terms.
9. Research is patient and unhurried activity.
10. The researcher is willing to follow his procedures to the conclusions that may be unpopular and bring social disapproval.
11. Research is carefully recorded and reported.
12. Conclusions and generalizations are arrived at carefully and cautiously.

Specific Characteristics of Research

The following are the main characteristics of research:

1. A Sound Philosophy of Social Studies as the Basis of Research

Robert R. Rusk observes. "In the application of scientific procedure to social studies a sound philosophy as well as a sound common sense must be invoked to save the scientific procedure from itself."

2. Research Is Based on Insight and Imagination

The same writer feels, "Social studies by its reliance on research must never fail to realize that in addition to its practical practitioner and skilled investigators, it stands in need of men and women of imaginative insight, who look beyond, he present and behold the vision splendid. If the vision would fade into the light of common day, not only will the people perish, but research itself will become a sterile futility."

3. Research Requires an Inter-Disciplinary Approach

Research is not the mere description of elementary and isolated facts of nature. It must be related to the study of complex relationships of various facts. It requires an inter- disciplinary approach.

4. Research Usually Employs Deductive Reasoning Process

Eric Hylla writes in the 'Nature and Functions of Research,' the science of mind commonly uses methods of description, explanation, interpretation, sympathetic or intuitive understanding methods which are mainly speculative and deductive in character and which rarely furnish results that can be subjected to measurement or mathematical procedures.

5. Research Should Come out of a Desire to Do Things Better

Stephen M. Corey writes. "Better social studies means better development or formulation of instructional aims, better motivation of pupils, better teaching methods, better evaluation and better supervision and administration, these are 'activities' or 'operations.'

6. Research Is Not as Exact as Research in Physical Science

No two human beings have ever been found to be alike. No scientific investigations of human behavior even those of so called "identical twins" have resulted in the findings of individuals completely similar in structure or behaviour. "In the whole world there are probably no two things exactly alike similarly no two human beings are alike, they differ physically in size, weight, height, colour of eyes and hair texture of skin and in a thousand other details as well as in thousands of details of mental, social and spiritual life," writes H.C. McKown. This fact stands in the way of making research as an exact science.

7. Research Is Not the Field of the Specialist Only

W.C. Redford writes, "In sum, I believe the teachers in every country have the opportunity and the capacity to undertake some research. Such research, carried out in the day-to-day work of the school, should be concerned directly with the problems of that school. It can properly concern itself with such matters as child development, class organisation, teacher-pupil relationships, interaction with the community, curriculum matters, teaching techniques and many others."

8. Research Generally Requires Inexpensive Material

In many social studies research studies we simply need subjects, i.e., children, their social studies, tools of daily use, paper and pencil and a few tests.

9. Research Is Based on the Subjectivity and Intangibility of Social Phenomena

Lundberg has pointed out that the physical phenomena may be known directly through sense, whereas social phenomena are known only symbolically through words representing such phenomena as tradition, custom, attitude, values and the whole realm of so called subjective worlds.

10. Research Is Perhaps Incapable of Being Dealt through Empirical Method

According to Lundberg "Exact science tends to become increasingly quantitative in its units, measures, and terminology while most of the matter of social science is quantitative and does not admit of quantitative statement. We can talk of urbanization, cultural assimilation etc. but we can't measure quantitatively. We may talk of growing indiscipline, but unless we can measure it, unless we can certain the degree of indiscipline, we cannot find a perfect cure."

11. Research Is Based on Inter Dependence of Causes and Effect

In case of a social phenomena the cause and the effect are inter dependent and one stimulates the other. It becomes, therefore, very difficult to find as to what is the cause and what is the fore effect. MacIver rightly points out, "Social science has hitherto suffered greatly from the attempt to make it conform to method derived from the order and more abstract sciences. It has led us to look for impossible results and to be disappointed at not getting them. We enquire, for example, after the manner of physical sciences which of the two related social phenomena is cause and which the effect. It usually turns out in the social sphere, that both are cause and both are effect."

12. Research Cannot Be a Mechanical Process

Research can never be made a mechanical process. There is no problem worthy of study that does not include unknown elements and does not require a fresh approach and attack. Too much of the research done by students in recent years has marked of the mechanical or merely following the methods and procedures of some predecessors without clear insight, into the problem itself or the methods to be used in attacking it. Much of the research in social studies that is being published fails to receive recognition because it lacks that spark of originality that must accompany an attack on a new problem.

Research methods and techniques can be taught, but after they are mastered there is still the problem of attacking a new problem and genuine contribution to social studies cannot be made without the willingness to pioneer into new fields or to work out new procedures. Genuine research must be an exploration. Any student who wishes to undertake research in social studies must be willing to take venture into the unknown and only by doing so he will bring back the fruit of genuine discovery.

Philosophy of Research

Research appears as something very abstract and complicated but on closer observation it is found that research fits together and is not as complicated as it may seem at first glance. A research study has a well known structure – a beginning, middle and an end. Before the modern idea of research emerged there is a term what philosophers used to call research – logical reasoning.

Based on the assumptions about how the world is perceived and how we can best come to understand it, we consider two major philosophical schools of thought – Positivism and Post –positivism. These are essentially important perspectives for contemporary social research. There are several other perspectives like relativism, subjectivism, constructivism, feminism etc.

Positivism & Post-Positivism

In its broadest sense, positivism is a rejection of metaphysics. It is a position that holds that the goal of knowledge is simply to describe the phenomena that we experience. The purpose of science is simply to stick to what we can observe and measure. Knowledge of anything beyond that, a positivist would hold, is impossible.

In a positivist view of the world, science was seen as the way to get at truth, to understand the world well enough so that we might predict and control it. The world and the universe were deterministic – they operated by laws of cause and effect that we could discern if we applied the unique approach of the scientific method. Science was largely a mechanistic or mechanical affair. We use deductive reasoning to postulate theories that we can test. Based on the results of our studies, we may learn that our theory doesn't fit the facts well and so we need to revise our theory to better predict reality. The positivist believed in *empiricism* – the idea that observation and measurement was the core of the scientific endeavor. The key approach of the scientific method is the experiment, the attempt to discern natural laws through direct manipulation and observation.

Post-positivism is a wholesale rejection of the central tenets of positivism. A post-positivist might begin by recognizing that the way scientists think and work and the way we think in our everyday life are not distinctly different. Scientific reasoning and common sense reasoning are essentially the same process. There is no difference in kind between the two, only a difference in degree. Scientists, for example, follow specific procedures to assure that observations are verifiable, accurate and consistent. In everyday reasoning, we don't always proceed so carefully (although, if you think about it, when the stakes are high, even in everyday life we become much more cautious about measurement. Think of the way most responsible parents keep continuous watch over their infants, noticing details that non-parents would never detect).

One of the most common forms of post-positivism is a philosophy called **critical realism**. A critical realist believes that there is a reality independent of our thinking about it that science can study.

Ethics in Research

We are going through a time of profound change in our understanding of the ethics of applied social research. From the time immediately after World War II until the early 1990s, there was a gradually developing consensus about the key ethical principles that should underlie the research endeavor. Two marker events stand out (among many others) as symbolic of this consensus. The Nuremberg War Crimes Trial following World War II brought to public view the ways German scientists had used captive human subjects as subjects in oftentimes gruesome experiments. Events like these forced the reexamination of ethical standards and the gradual development of a consensus that potential human subjects needed to be protected from being used as 'guinea pigs' in scientific research.

By the 1990s, the dynamics of the situation changed. Cancer patients and persons with AIDS fought publicly with the medical research establishment about the long time needed to get approval for and complete research into potential cures for fatal diseases. In many cases, it is the ethical assumptions of the previous thirty years that drive this 'go-slow' mentality. After all, we would rather risk denying treatment for a while until we achieve enough confidence in a treatment, rather than run the risk of harming innocent people (as in the Nuremberg events). But now, those who were threatened with fatal illness were saying to the research establishment that they *wanted* to be test subjects, even under experimental conditions of considerable risk. You had several very vocal and articulate patient groups who wanted to be experimented on coming up against an ethical review system that was designed to protect them from being experimented on.

Although the last few years in the ethics of research have been tumultuous ones, it is beginning to appear that a new consensus is evolving that involves the stakeholder groups most affected by a problem participating more actively in the formulation of guidelines for research. While it's not entirely clear, at present, what the new consensus will be, it is almost certain that it will not fall at either extreme: protecting against human experimentation at all costs **vs.** allowing anyone who is willing to be experimented on.

Research Fallacies

A *fallacy* is an error in reasoning, usually based on mistaken assumptions. Researchers are very familiar with all the ways they could go wrong, with the fallacies they are susceptible to. There are two important fallacies -

The **Ecological Fallacy** occurs when you make conclusions about individuals based only on analyses of group data. For instance, assume that you measured the math scores of a particular classroom and found that they had the highest average score in the district. Later (probably at the mall) you run into one of the kids from that class and you think to yourself "she must be a math whiz." That is a fallacy Just because she comes from the class with the highest *average* doesn't mean that she is automatically a high-scorer in math. She could be the lowest math scorer in a class that otherwise consists of math geniuses

An **Exception Fallacy** is sort of the reverse of the ecological fallacy. It occurs when you reach a group conclusion on the basis of exceptional cases. This is the kind of fallacious reasoning that happens when a person who sees a woman make a driving error and concludes that "women are terrible drivers." This is also a fallacy.

Both of these fallacies point to some of the traps that exist in both research and everyday reasoning. They also point out how important it is that we do research. We need to determine empirically how individuals perform (not just rely on group averages). Similarly, we need to look at whether there are correlations between certain behaviors and certain groups.

Motivating Factors of Social Science Research

There are six important motivating factors of social research. These are

(1) Stimulation of Respondent,

(2) Stimulation of Researcher,

(3) A Sense or Participation,

(4) Growth of Knowledge,

(5) Quest for Progress,

(6) Curiosity to Understand the Cause and Effect Relationship of Various Social Phenomena.

Stimulation of Respondent

As the researcher depends upon the respondents for collection of data for the attainment of the research objectives, one of the most important tasks of the researcher is to inspire and stimulate the respondents with zeal to help for the accomplishment of research goals. In other words the motivation of the respondents plays a significant role for the success of any kind of research.

Human motives are based on certain needs which may be primary or secondary and vary in their intensity according to situation and time. The researcher must study these needs, try to understand their intensity and have the responsibility to satisfy them in order to stimulate the respondents for research work.

Motivation means any idea, need, emotion or organic state that prompts a man to an action. Motivation is an internal factor that integrates a man's behaviour. As the motive is within the individual, it is necessary to study the needs, emotions etc. in order to motivate him to co-operate in the research work.

The following are the important inducing factors which influence the respondent's behaviour and induce him for the best performance to meet the need of research

a. The research should be directed towards the solution of respondents problem.
b. The nature of the problem or topic must have social relevance.
c. The respondent should clearly spell the goals of research.
d. The respondents much be informed about the matters concerning objectives of the research. The more a person knows about its subject matter the more interest and concern he will develop.
e. Respondents can be motivated to involve in research if they get continous recognition for their efforts. Respondents provide valuable information and suggestion for the success of research world.

If the researcher has a praise of words for the respondents cooperation, it motivates the respondents more and more to be involved in the research process. Thus recognition tends to motivate the respondents to provide information for research

Stimulation of Researcher

The success of a research work to a great extent depends upon the motivation of the researcher as well. The following are some of the factors which stimulate a researcher to conduct research effectively –

a. The researcher must have a concrete and complete knowledge of the subject under study. He must be capable of removing the doubts of the respondents regarding the study
b. He must have personal interest in the study undertaken.
c. The researcher must have sufficient knowledge about the respondents
d. The researcher must have the idea of the tools of research

A Sense of Participation

Participation in a research activity does not mean simply the involvement of the respondents in giving information on a topic or problem. In real sense, participation is an individual's mental and emotional involvement in research solutions that encourage him to contribute to research and to share responsibility for it.

From utilitarian points of view the main goal of research is to understand social life and attempt on social welfare. However it cannot be done without the active participation of the people involved in the process of social research.

Any social research whether it is meant for the development of a specific section of society or for the overall development of the entire society, requires participation of people. Research does not only mean involvement of the researcher but it also requires the conscious participation of the respondents.

The respondents involve themselves in thinking, identifying the needs, fixing priorities of the needs, providing valuable information, implementing and evaluating critically various research programmes. Thus it involves the participation of both the researcher and the respondents.

Growth of Knowledge

Interest for increasing knowledge motivates people to do research in their own field. Research adds to the existing knowledge in a systematic way. The quest for knowledge is therefore an important motivating factor in social research. Discovering the truth always forces man to undertake research in own society.

Quest for Progress

Research has proved to be a significant and powerful tool in bringing social progress. Without scientific social research there would be very little progress. The results of social research will provide us with the possible means to bring solution to different social problems. Research opens new avenues and provide a better alternative to us. It enhances the efficiency of all the agencies and organizations engaged in the development of society. So the quest for progress is also another motivating factor of social research.

1. **Curiosity to Understand the Cause and Effect Relationship of Various Social Phenomenon**: Research is nothing but a desire to understand the causal explanation of various facts and to explain the natural laws which govern them. Social research tries to discover the cause – effect relationship between different aspects of a social phenomenon. In order to solve a social problem one must first understand the root cause of that particular problem. Finding the cause of an effect is one of the greatest tasks of research and its quest always motivation people to understand research.

Chapter 2

Nature of Research

In order to understand the nature of research it is essential to know the basic components of research. Components of research study are discussed in terms of components of a research proposal and components of a thesis.

Components of a Study

Basic Components of a Research Proposal

Title/Cover Page	
Acknowledgements (Optional)	
Abstract	
Table of Contents	
List of tables (required if your proposal contains tables)	**Front Pages**
List of Figures (required if your proposal contains figures)	
Acronyms/Abbreviations (If any)	
Operational definitions (If any)	

1. Introduction	
1.1 Back ground of the study	
1.2 Statement of the problem	
1.3 Research Objectives	
1.4 Significance of the study	
1.5 Scope of the study	
1.6 Limitations of the study	
2. Literature Review	
3. Research method	
3.1 Research Type Approach	
3.2 Sampling	**Body of the text**
3.2.1 Target population, the context and units of analysis	
3.2.2 Sampling method	
3.3 Sources of Data	
3.4 Data collection method	
3.5 Variables and measurement/measures	
3.6 Methods of data analysis	
4. Structure/Organization of the paper	
5. Research schedule and budget requested (if any)	
5.1 Research schedule	
5.2 Research budget	
References	**End Pages**
Appendices (Optional)	

Brief Components of a Thesis

Title/Cover Page	Front papers/matters
Declaration Page	
Board of Examiners approval sheet	
Acknowledgements	
Abstract	
Table of Contents	
List of Tables (Required if your thesis contains Tables)	
List of Figures (Required if your thesis contains Figures)	
Acronyms	
Operational definitions	
Structure of the thesis	
Chapter 1 – introduction	Body of the Text
1.1 Background of the study	
1.2 Statement of the problem	
1.3 Research Objectives	
1.4 Significance of the study	
1.5 Scope of the study	
1.6 Limitations of the study	
Chapter 2 – Literature Review	
Chapter 3 – Research methods	
Chapter 4 – Data Analysis and Interpretation	
Chapter 5 – Conclusions and recommendations	
References	End matters
Appendices	

Note: There are several different styles of referencing:

- APA

APA (American Psychological Association) style is most frequently used within the social sciences, in order to cite various sources.

This **APA** Citation Guide, revised according to the 6th edition of the **APA** manual, provides the general format for in-text citations and the **reference** page.

- MLA

Modern Language Association (**MLA**) Style Guide. The **MLA** system uses in-text **citations** rather than footnotes or endnotes. The **citations** in-text are very brief, usually just the author's family name and a relevant page number.

- Oxford

The **Oxford Referencing** style is a note citation system. It is also sometimes referred to as a documentary-note style. It has two components: Footnote Citation. **Reference** List.

- Harvard

Harvard uses the 'author-date' **style of referencing**. That is, in-text references (generally) appear in the following **format**: (Author's Last Name Year of Publication, Page Number(s)) Example: (Austen 1813, p. 64)

- Chicago

The *Chicago manual of style* sets out two referencing systems: footnotes and a bibliography, and an author-date system similar to APA.

Types of Research

The basic types of research are as follows:

(i) ***Descriptive vs. Analytical***: *Descriptive research* includes surveys and fact-finding enquiries of different kinds. The major purpose of descriptive research is description of the state of affairs as it exists at present. In social science and business research we quite often use the term *Ex post facto research* for descriptive research studies. The main characteristic of this method is that the researcher has no control over the variables; he can only report what has happened or what is happening. Most *ex post facto research* projects are used for descriptive studies in which the researcher seeks to measure such items as, for example, frequency of shopping, preferences of people, or similar data. *Ex post facto studies* also include attempts by researchers to discover causes even when they cannot control the variables. The methods of research utilized in descriptive research are survey methods of all kinds, including comparative and correlational methods.

In *analytical research*, on the other hand, the researcher has to use facts or information already available, and analyze these to make a critical evaluation of the material.

(ii) **Applied vs. Fundamental**: Research can either be applied (or action) research or fundamental (to basic or pure) research. *Applied research* aims at finding a solution for an immediate problem facing a society or an industrial/business organization, whereas *fundamental research* is mainly concerned with generalisations and with the formulation of a theory. "Gathering knowledge for knowledge's sake is termed 'pure' or 'basic' research." Research concerning some natural phenomenon or relating to pure mathematics are examples of fundamental research. Similarly, research studies, concerning human behavior carried on with a view to make generalisations about human behavior, are also examples of fundamental research, but research aimed at certain conclusions (say, a solution) facing a concrete social or business problem is an example of applied research. Research to identify social, economic or political trends that may affect a particular institution or the marketing research or evaluation research are examples of applied research.

(iii) **Quantitative vs. Qualitative**: Quantitative research is based on the measurement of quantity or amount. It is applicable to phenomena that can be expressed in terms of quantity. Qualitative research, on the other hand, is concerned with qualitative phenomenon, i.e., phenomena relating to or involving quality or kind. For instance, when we are interested in investigating the reasons for human behavior (i.e., why people think or do certain things), Qualitative research is specially important in the behavioral sciences where the aim is to discover the underlying motives of human behavior. Through such research we can analyze the various factors which motivate people to behave in a particular manner or which make people like or dislike a particular thing.

(iv) ***Conceptual vs. Empirical***: Conceptual research is that related to some abstract idea(s) or theory. It is generally used by philosophers and thinkers to develop new concepts or to reinterpret existing ones. On the other hand, empirical research relies on experience or observation alone, often without due regard for system and theory. It is data-based research, coming up with conclusions which are capable of being verified by observation or experiment. We can also call it as experimental type of research. In such a research it is necessary to get at facts firsthand, at their source, and actively to go about doing certain things to stimulate the production of desired information. In such a research, the researcher must first provide himself with a working hypothesis or guess as to the probable results. He then works to get enough facts (data) to prove or disprove his hypothesis.

(v) ***Some Other Types of Research***: All other types of research are variations of one or more of the above stated approaches, based on either the purpose of research, or the time required to accomplish research, on the environment in which research is done, or on the basis of some other similar factor. Form the point of view of time, we can think of research either as ***one-time research or longitudinal research.*** In the former case the research is confined to a single time-period, whereas in the latter case the research is carried on over several time-periods.

Research can be ***field-setting research or laboratory research or simulation research***, depending upon the environment in which it is to be carried out.

Research can as well be understood as ***clinical or diagnostic research***. Such research follow case-study methods or in-depth approaches to reach the basic causal relations. Such studies usually go deep into the causes of things or events that interest us, using very small samples and very deep probing data gathering devices.

The research may be ***exploratory* or it may be *formalized***. The objective of exploratory research is the development of hypotheses rather than their testing, whereas formalized research studies are those with substantial structure and with specific hypotheses to be tested.

Historical Research is that which utilizes historical sources like documents, remains, etc. to study events or ideas of the past, including the philosophy of persons and groups at any remote point of time.

Research can also be classified as **conclusion-oriented** and **decision-oriented**. While doing conclusion oriented research, a researcher is free to pick up a problem, redesign the enquiry as he proceeds and is prepared to conceptualize as he wishes. Decision-oriented research is always for the need of a decision maker and the researcher in this case is not free to embark upon research according to his own inclination. Operations research is an example of decision oriented research since it is a scientific method of providing executive departments with a quantitative basis for decisions regarding operations under their control.

Research Approaches

The above description of the types of research brings to light the fact that there are two basic approaches to research, viz., *quantitative approach* and the *qualitative approach*. The former involves the generation of data in quantitative form which can be subjected to rigorous quantitative analysis in a formal and rigid fashion. This approach can be further sub-classified into *inferential, experimental* and *simulation approaches* to research. The purpose of *inferential approach* to research is to form a data base from which to infer characteristics or relationships of population. This usually means survey research where a sample of population is studied (questioned or observed) to determine its characteristics, and it is then inferred that the population has the same characteristics.

Experimental approach is characterized by much greater control over the research environment and in this case some variables are manipulated to observe their effect on other variables. *Simulation approach* involves the construction of an artificial environment within which relevant information and data can be generated. This permits an observation of the dynamic behaviour of a system (or its sub-system) under controlled conditions.

Qualitative approach to research is concerned with subjective assessment of attitudes, opinions and behavior. Research in such a situation is a function of researcher's insights and impressions. Such an approach to research generates results either in non-quantitative form or in the form which are not subjected to rigorous quantitative analysis. Generally, the techniques of focus group interviews, projective techniques and depth interviews are used.

Research Methods versus Methodology

Research methods may be understood as all those methods/techniques that are used for conduction of research, *thus, refer to the methods the researchers use in performing research operations*. In other words, all those methods which are used by the researcher during the course of studying his research problem are termed as research methods.

Since the object of research it to arrive at a solution for a given problem, the available data and the unknown aspects of the problem have to be related to each other to make a solution possible. Keeping this in view, research methods can be put into the following three groups:

1. In the first group we include those methods which are concerned with the collection of data. These methods will be used where the data already available are not sufficient to arrive at the required solution;
2. The second group consists of those statistical techniques which are used for establishing relationships between the data and the unknowns;
3. The third group consists of those methods which are used to evaluate the accuracy of the results obtained.

Research methods falling in the above stated last two groups are generally taken as the analytical tools of research.

Research methodology is a way to systematically solve the research problem. It may be understood as a science of studying how research is done scientifically. In it we study the various steps that are generally adopted by a researcher in studying his research problem along with the logic behind them. It is necessary for the researcher to know not only the research methods/techniques but also the methodology. Researchers not only need to know how to develop certain indices or tests, how to calculate the mean, the mode, the median or the standard deviation or chi-square, how to apply particular research techniques, but they also need to know which of these methods or techniques, are relevant and which are not, and what would they mean and indicate and why.

Researchers also need to understand the assumptions underlying various techniques and they need to know the criteria by which they can decide that certain techniques and procedures will be applicable to certain problems and others will not. All this means that it is necessary for the researcher to design his methodology for his problem as the same may differ from problem to problem.

For example, an architect, who designs a building, has to consciously evaluate the basis of his decisions, i.e., he has to evaluate why and on what basis he selects particular size, number and location of doors, windows and ventilators, uses particular materials and not others and the like. Similarly, in research the scientist has to expose the research decisions to evaluation before they are implemented. He has to specify very clearly and precisely what decisions he selects and why he selects them so that they can be evaluated by others also.

The scope of research methodology is wider than that of research methods. Thus, when we talk of research methodology we not only talk of the research methods but also consider the logic behind the methods we use in the context of our research study and explain why we are using a particular method or technique and why we are not using others so that research results are capable of being evaluated either by the researcher himself or by others.

Why a research study has been undertaken, how the research problem has been defined, in what way and why the hypothesis has been formulated, what data have been collected and what particular method has been adopted, why particular technique of analysing data has been used and a host of similar other questions are usually answered when we talk of research methodology concerning a research problem or study.

Major Steps in Conducting Research

Research process consists of series of actions or steps necessary to effectively carry out research and the desired sequencing of these steps. The chart shown in the following Figure illustrates a research process.

RESEARCH PROCESS IN FLOW CHART

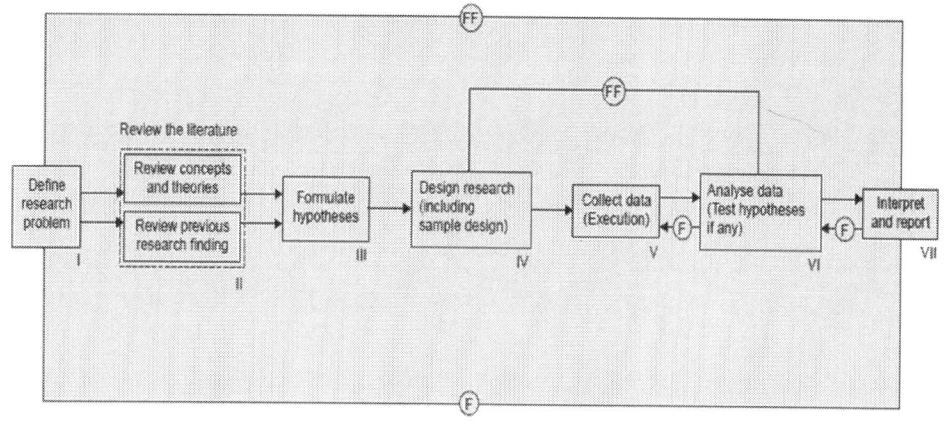

Where F = feed back (Helps in controlling the sub-system to which it is transmitted)
FF = feed forward (Serves the vital function of providing criteria for evaluation)

The following are the various steps followed in research process:

1. Formulating the research problem;
2. Extensive literature survey;
3. Developing the hypothesis;
4. Preparing the research design;
5. Determining sample design;
6. Collecting the data;
7. Execution of the project;
8. Analysis of data;
9. Hypothesis testing;
10. Generalizations and interpretation, and
11. Preparation of the report or presentation of the results, i.e., formal write-up of conclusions reached.

1. **Formulating the Research Problem:** There are two types of research problems, viz., those which relate to states of nature and those which relate to relationships between variables. At the very outset the researcher must single out the problem

he wants to study, i.e., he must decide the general area of interest or aspect of a subject-matter that he would like to inquire into. Initially the problem may be stated in a broad general way and then the ambiguities, if any, relating to the problem be resolved. Then, the feasibility of a particular solution has to be considered before a working formulation of the problem can be set up. The formulation of a general topic into a specific research problem, thus, constitutes the first step in a scientific enquiry.

Essentially two steps are involved in formulating the research problem, viz., understanding the problem thoroughly, and rephrasing the same into meaningful terms from an analytical point of view. In an academic institution the researcher can seek the help from a guide who is usually an experienced man and has several research problems in mind. Often, the guide puts forth the problem in general terms and it is up to the researcher to narrow it down and phrase the problem in operational terms.

The researcher must at the same time examine all available literature to get himself acquainted with the selected problem. He may review two types of literature—the conceptual literature concerning the concepts and theories, and the empirical literature consisting of studies made earlier which are similar to the one proposed. The basic outcome of this review will be the knowledge as to what data and other materials are available for operational purposes which will enable the researcher to specify his own research problem in a meaningful context. After this the researcher rephrases the problem into analytical or operational terms i.e., to put the problem in as specific terms as possible.

This task of formulating, or defining, a research problem is a step of greatest importance in the entire research process. The problem to be investigated must be defined unambiguously for that will help discriminating relevant data from irrelevant ones. Care must, however, be taken to verify the objectivity and validity of the background facts concerning the problem.

2. **Extensive Literature Survey:** Once the problem is formulated, a brief summary of it should be written down. The earlier studies,

if any, which are similar to the study in hand should be carefully studied. A good library will be a great help to the researcher at this stage. There are two types of literature—the conceptual literature concerning the concepts and theories, and the empirical literature consisting of studies made earlier which are similar to the one proposed.

3. **Development of Working Hypotheses:** After extensive literature survey, researcher should state in clear terms the working hypothesis or hypotheses. Working hypothesis is tentative assumption made in order to draw out and test its logical or empirical consequences. As such the manner in which research hypotheses are developed is particularly important since they provide the focal point for research. They also affect the manner in which tests must be conducted in the analysis of data and indirectly the quality of data which is required for the analysis. Hypothesis should be very specific and limited to the piece of research in hand because it has to be tested. The role of the hypothesis is to guide the researcher by delimiting the area of research and to keep him on the right track.

4. **Preparing the Research Design:** The research problem having been formulated in clear cut terms, the researcher will be required to prepare a research design, i.e., he will have to state the conceptual structure within which research would be conducted. The function of research design is to provide for the collection of relevant evidence with minimal expenditure of effort, time and money. But how all these can be achieved depends mainly on the research purpose.

Research purposes may be grouped into four categories, viz., (i) Exploration, (ii) Description, (iii) Diagnosis, and (iv) Experimentation. A flexible research design which provides opportunity for considering many different aspects of a problem is considered appropriate if the purpose of the research study is that of exploration. But when the purpose happens to be an accurate description of a situation or of an association between variables, the suitable design will be one that minimises bias and maximises the reliability of the data collected and analyzed.

There are several research designs, such as, experimental and non-experimental hypothesis testing. Experimental designs can be either informal designs (such as before-and-after without control, after-only with control, before-and-after with control) or formal designs (such as completely randomized design, randomized block design, Latin square design, simple and complex factorial designs), out of which the researcher must select one for his own project.

The preparation of the research design, appropriate for a particular research problem, involves usually the consideration of the following:

(i) The means of obtaining the information;

(ii) The availability and skills of the researcher and his staff (if any);

(iii) Explanation of the way in which selected means of obtaining information will be organized and the reasoning leading to the selection;

(iv) The time available for research; and

(v) The cost factor relating to research, i.e., the finance available for the purpose.

5. **Determining Sample Design:** All the items under consideration in any field of inquiry constitute a 'universe' or 'population.' A complete enumeration of all the items in the 'population' is known as a census inquiry. It can be presumed that in such an inquiry when all the items are covered no element of chance is left and highest accuracy is obtained. But in practice this may not be true. Even the slightest element of bias in such an inquiry will get larger and larger as the number of observations increases. Moreover, there is no way of checking the element of bias or its extent except through a resurvey or use of sample checks. Besides, this type of inquiry involves a great deal of time, money and energy. Not only this, census inquiry is not possible in practice under many circumstances. For instance, blood testing is done only on sample basis. Hence, quite often we select only a few items from the universe for our study purposes. The items so selected constitute what is technically called a sample.

The researcher must decide the way of selecting a sample or what is popularly known as the sample design. In other words, a sample design is a definite plan determined before any data are actually collected for obtaining a sample from a given population.. Samples can be either probability samples or non-probability samples. With probability samples each element has a known probability of being included in the sample but the non-probability samples do not allow the researcher to determine this probability. Probability samples are those based on simple random sampling, systematic sampling, stratified sampling, cluster/area sampling whereas non-probability samples are those based on convenience sampling, judgment sampling and quota sampling techniques.

A brief mention of the important sample designs is as follows:

(i) *Deliberate Sampling*: Deliberate sampling is also known as purposive or non-probability sampling. This sampling method involves purposive or deliberate selection of particular units of the universe for constituting a sample which represents the universe. When population elements are selected for inclusion in the sample based on the ease of access, it can be called *convenience sampling*. On the other hand, in *judgement sampling* the researcher's judgement is used for selecting items which he considers as representative of the population.

(ii) *Simple Random Sampling*: This type of sampling is also known as chance sampling or probability sampling where each and every item in the population has an equal chance of inclusion in the sample and each one of the possible samples, in case of finite universe, has the same probability of being selected. For example, if we have to select a sample of 300 items from a universe of 15,000 items, then we can put the names or numbers of all the 15,000 items on slips of paper and conduct a lottery.

(iii) *Systematic Sampling*: In some instances the most practical way of sampling is to select e very 15th name on a list, every 10th house on one side of a street and so on. Sampling of this type is known as systematic sampling. An element of randomness is usually introduced into this kind of sampling by using random numbers to pick up the unit with which to start. This procedure is useful when sampling frame is available in the form of a list. In such a design the selection process starts by picking some random point in the list and then every nth element is selected until the desired number is secured.

(iv) *Stratified Sampling:* If the population from which a sample is to be drawn does not constitute a homogeneous group, then stratified sampling technique is applied so as to obtain a representative sample. In this technique, the population is stratified into a number of non-overlapping subpopulations or strata and sample items are selected from each stratum. If the items selected from each stratum is based on simple random sampling the entire procedure, first stratification and then simple random sampling, is known as *stratified random sampling.*

(v) *Quota Sampling:* In stratified sampling the cost of taking random samples from individual strata is often so expensive that interviewers are simply given quota to be filled from different strata, the actual selection of items for sample being left to the interviewer's judgment. This is called quota sampling. The size of the quota for each stratum is generally proportionate to the size of that stratum in the population. Quota sampling is thus an important form of non-probability sampling. Quota samples generally happen to be judgment samples rather than random samples.

(vi) *Cluster Sampling and Area Sampling:* Cluster sampling involves grouping the population and then selecting the groups or the clusters rather than individual elements for inclusion in the sample.

(vii) *Multi-Stage Sampling:* This is a further development of the idea of cluster sampling. This technique is meant for big inquiries extending to a considerably large geographical area like an entire country. Under multi-stage sampling the first stage may be to select large primary sampling units such as states, then districts, then towns and finally certain families. If the technique of random-sampling is applied the sampling procedure is described as multi-sampling.

(viii) *Sequential Sampling:* This is somewhat a complex sample design where the ultimate size of the sample is not fixed in advance but is determined according to mathematical decisions on the basis of information yielded as survey progresses. This design is usually adopted under acceptance sampling plan in the context of statistical quality control. In practice, several of the methods of sampling described above may well be used in the same study in which case it can be called mixed sampling

6. **Collecting the Data:** There are several ways of collecting the appropriate data which differ considerably in context of money costs, time and other resources at the disposal of the researcher.

Primary data can be collected either through experiment or through survey. If the researcher conducts an experiment, he observes some quantitative measurements, or the data, with the help of which he examines the truth contained in his hypothesis. But in the case of a survey, data can be collected by any one or more of the following ways:

(i) *By Observation:* This method implies the collection of information by way of investigator's own observation, without interviewing the respondents. The information obtained relates to what is currently happening and is not complicated by either the past behaviour or future intentions or attitudes of respondents. This method is no doubt an expensive method and the information provided by this method is also very limited. As such this method is not suitable in inquiries where large samples are concerned.

(ii) *Through Personal Interview:* The investigator follows a rigid procedure and seeks answers to a set of pre-conceived questions through personal interviews. This method of collecting data is usually carried out in a structured way where output depends upon the ability of the interviewer to a large extent.

(iii) *Through Telephone Interviews:* This method of collecting information involves contacting the respondents on telephone itself. This is not a very widely used method but it plays an important role in industrial surveys in developed regions, particularly, when the survey has to be accomplished in a very limited time.

(iv) *By Mailing of Questionnaires:* The researcher and the respondents do come in contact with each other if this method of survey is adopted. Questionnaires are mailed to the respondents with a request to return after completing the same. It is the most extensively used method in various economic and business surveys. Before applying this method, usually a Pilot Study for testing the questionnaire is conduced which reveals the weaknesses, if any, of the questionnaire. Questionnaire to be used must be prepared very carefully so that it may prove to be effective in collecting the relevant information.

(v) *Through Schedules:* Under this method the enumerators are appointed and given training. They are provided with schedules containing relevant questions. These enumerators go to respondents with these schedules. Data are collected by filling up the schedules by enumerators on the basis of replies given by respondents. Much depends upon the capability of enumerators so far as this method is concerned. Some occasional field checks on the work of the enumerators may ensure sincere work.

The researcher should select one of these methods of collecting the data taking into consideration the nature of investigation, objective and scope of the inquiry, financial resources, available time and the desired degree of accuracy.

7. **Execution of the Project:** Execution of the project is a very important step in the research process. If the execution of the project proceeds on correct lines, the data to be collected would be adequate and dependable. The researcher should see that the project is executed in a systematic manner and in time. If the survey is to be conducted by means of structured questionnaires, data can

be readily machine-processed. In such a situation, questions as well as the possible answers may be coded. If the data are to be collected through interviewers, arrangements should be made for proper selection and training of the interviewers. The training may be given with the help of instruction manuals which explain clearly the job of the interviewers at each step. Occasional field checks should be made to ensure that the interviewers are doing their assigned job sincerely and efficiently.

8. **Analysis of Data:** After the data have been collected, the researcher turns to the task of analyzing them. The analysis of data requires a number of closely related operations such as establishment of categories, the application of these categories to raw data through coding, tabulation and then drawing statistical inferences. The unwieldy data should necessarily be condensed into a few manageable groups and tables for further analysis. Thus, researcher should classify the raw data into some purposeful and usable categories.

Coding operation is usually done at this stage through which the categories of data are transformed into symbols that may be tabulated and counted.

Editing is the procedure that improves the quality of the data for coding. With coding the stage is ready for tabulation.

Tabulation is a part of the technical procedure wherein the classified data are put in the form of tables. The mechanical devices can be made use of at this juncture.

Analysis work after tabulation is generally based on the computation of various percentages, coefficients, etc., by applying various well defined statistical formulae. In the process of analysis, relationships or differences supporting or conflicting with original or new hypotheses should be subjected to tests of significance to determine with what validity data can be said to indicate any conclusion(s).

9. **Hypothesis-Testing:** After analysing the data as stated above, the researcher is in a position to test the hypotheses, if any, he had formulated earlier. Do the facts support the hypotheses or they

happen to be contrary? This is the usual question which should be answered while testing hypotheses. Various tests, such as Chi square test, *t*-test, *F*-test, have been developed by statisticians for the purpose. The hypotheses may be tested through the use of one or more of such tests, depending upon the nature and object of research inquiry. Hypothesis-testing will result in either accepting the hypothesis or in rejecting it. If the researcher had no hypotheses to start with, generalizations established on the basis of data may be stated as hypotheses to be tested by subsequent researches in times to come.

10. **Generalisations and Interpretation:** If a hypothesis is tested and upheld several times, it may be possible for the researcher to arrive at generalisation, i.e., to build a theory. As a matter of fact, the real value of research lies in its ability to arrive at certain generalisations. If the researcher had no hypothesis to start with, he might seek to explain his findings on the basis of some theory. It is known as interpretation. The process of interpretation may quite often trigger off new questions which in turn may lead to further researches.

11. **Preparation of the Report or the Thesis:** Finally, the researcher has to prepare the report of what has been done by him. Writing of report must be done with great care keeping in view the following:

    1. The layout of the report should be as follows: (*i*) the preliminary pages; (*ii*) the main text, and (*iii*) the end matter.

        In its preliminary pages the report should carry title and date followed by acknowledgements and foreword. Then there should be a table of contents followed by a list of tables and list of graphs and charts, if any, given in the report.

        The main text of the report should have the following parts:

        (a) *Introduction:* It should contain a clear statement of the objective of the research and an explanation of the methodology adopted in accomplishing the research. The scope of the study along with various limitations should as well be stated in this part.

(b) *Summary of findings:* After introduction there would appear a statement of findings and recommendations in non-technical language. If the findings are extensive, they should be summarised.

(c) *Main report:* The main body of the report should be presented in logical sequence and broken-down into readily identifiable sections.

(d) *Conclusion:* Towards the end of the main text, researcher should again put down the results of his research clearly and precisely. In fact, it is the final summing up.

At the end of the report, appendices should be enlisted in respect of all technical data. Bibliography, i.e., list of books, journals, reports, etc., consulted, should also be given in the end. Index should also be given specially in a published research report.

2. Report should be written in a concise and objective style in simple language avoiding vague expressions such as 'it seems,' 'there may be,' and the like.

3. Charts and illustrations in the main report should be used only if they present the information more clearly and forcibly.

4. Calculated 'confidence limits' must be mentioned and the various constraints experienced in conducting research operations may as well be stated.

Chapter 3

Identifying Research Problem

Research Problem?

A research problem, in general, refers to some difficulty which a researcher experiences in the context of either a theoretical or practical situation and wants to obtain a solution for the same.

A research problem is a definite or clear expression [statement] about an area of concern, a condition to be improved upon, a difficulty to be eliminated, or a troubling question that exists in scholarly literature, in theory, or within existing practice that points to a need for meaningful understanding and deliberate.

According to Kerlinger, "A problem is an interrogative sentence or statement that asks what relation exists between two or more variables. The answer to question will provide what is having sought in the research."

Identification of Research Problem

The identification and analyzing a research problem is the first and most crucial step of research process. A problem cannot be solved effectively unless a researcher possesses the intellect and insight to isolate and understand the specific factors giving rise to the difficulty.

The present research scholars understand that identification of a problem means to select a topic of a research or statement of the problem. It is wrong to think so. A topic or statement of the problem and research problem are not the synonymous but they are inclusive. The problem concerns with the functioning of the broader area of field studied whereas a topic or title or statement of the problem is the verbal statement of the problem. The topic is the definition of the problem which delimits or pin points the task of a researcher.

It is the usual practice of the researches that they select the topic of the study from different sources especially from research abstracts. They do not identify the problem, but a problem is made on the basis of the topic. It results that the researcher has no involvement in his research activities.

Whatever they do, do mechanically. Since identifying the exact nature and dimensions of a problem is of major importance in research work, it is very essential that an investigator should learn how to recognize and define a problem. He should proceed step by step in locating the research problem. The following steps are to be followed in identifying a research problem:

Steps Involved in Identifying a Research Problem

Step 1: Determining the field of research in which a researcher is keen to do the research work.

Step 2: The researcher should develop the mastery on the area or it should be the field of his specialization.

Step 3: He should review the researchers conducted in area to know the recent trend and studies in the area.

Step 4: On the basis of review, he should consider the priority field of the study.

Step 5: He should draw an analogy and insight in identifying a problem or employ his personal experience of the field in locating the problem. He may take help of supervisor or expertee of the field.

Step 6: He should pin-point specific aspect of the problem which is to be investigated.

For example a researcher wants to work in the field of teacher-education which is the field of his interest. He has the deep insight and mastery over the area. On the basis of review and his personal experience, the researcher perceives a problem in the field of teacher-education programme that training institutions and colleges of education are not able to produce effective teachers although large number of such institutions have been opened. This problem has the several dimensions but these can be studied simultaneously. The researcher further visualizes that the potential candidates are not admitted in this programme. A question arises: Are the potential candidates admitted in our teacher education problem? Thus, the procedure of identification of a problem can be shown with the help of a paradigm.

The following are the major tasks to be performed in analyzing a problematic situation as given below:

1. Accumulating the facts that might be related to the problem.
2. Setting by observations whether the facts are relevant.
3. Tracing any relationship between facts that might reveal the key to the difficulty.
4. Proposing various explanations for the cause or the difficulty.
5. Ascertaining through observations and analysis whether these explanations are relevant to the problem.
6. Tracing relationship between explanations that may give an insight into the problem solution.
7. Tracing relationship between facts and explanations.
8. Questioning assumptions underlying the analysis of the problem.
9. Tracing the irrelevant facts which are not concerned with the problem.
10. Locating the irrelevant explanations which are not related to the problem.

After going through these processes, the researcher will be able to define or state the problem.

Sources of Problem

The selection of a suitable problem is not an easy task. It is a serious responsibility to commit oneself to a problem that will inevitably require much time and energy and which is so academically significant.

The following are the main sources to which one may proceed for a suitable research problem:

1. Personal experiences of the investigator in his field are the main source for identifying suitable problem. Many of the problems

confronted in the classroom, the school or the community lend themselves to investigation and they are perhaps more appropriate for the beginning researcher than are problems more remote from his own teaching experiences.

2. The other source of problem which is most frequently used by the investigator as suggested by the supervisors, is the extensive study of available literature-research abstracts, journals, hand-books of research international abstracts etc. He can draw an analogy for selecting a research problem or can think parallel problem in the field studied.

3. In the choice of a suitable problem, the researcher has to decide his field of investigation. He should study the field intensively in the specific area, this may enable him to identify a problem from the specific field.

4. The new innovations, technological changes and curricular developments are constantly bringing new problems and new-opportunities for Social Studies Research.

5. The most practical source of problem is to consult supervisor, experts of the field and most experienced person of the field. They may suggest most significant problem of the area. He can discuss certain issues of the area to emerge a problem.

6. It is a general practice that researchers suggest some problems in their research reports. The researcher can pick up a suitable problem for his own study.

Criteria for Selection of a Problem

The factors that are to be considered in the selection of a research problem include both the external and personal criteria. External criteria have to do with such matters as novelty and importance for the field availability of data and method, and institutional or administrative cooperation. Personal criteria involves such considerations as interest, training, cost and time, etc.

Thus criteria for the selection of the problem suggested by Good and Scates are as follows:

1. Novelty and avoidance of unnecessary duplications.

2. Importance for the field represented and implementation.
3. Interest, intellectual curiosity, and drive.
4. Training and personal qualifications.
5. Availability of data and method.
6. Special equipment and working conditions.
7. Approachability of the sample.
8. Sponsorship and administrative cooperation.
9. Hazards, penalties and handicaps.
10. Cost and returns.
11. Time factor.

1. Novelty and Avoidance of Unnecessary Duplication

The question of novelty or newness is not merely one of duplication of earlier investigations. It involves the regency of the data summarized especially in the case of survey studies made during a period of Economic, Educational and Social change.

2. Importance for the Field Represented and Implementation

This criterion of importance in choice of a problem involves such matters as significance for the field involved, timelines and practical value in term of application and implementation of the results. Scientific research in Education, psychology and social sciences in general have an especially urgent obligation to play a social role rendering service to society and humanity.

3. Interest, Intellectual Curiosity and Drive

One of the personal motives of research most frequently mentioned by scientists themselves is pure curiosity, accompanied by genuine interest and a derived satisfaction and enjoyment.

4. Availability of Data and Method

The data under consideration must meet certain standards of accuracy, objectivity and verifiability.

5. Special Equipment and Working Conditions

The major purpose of equipment is to define the process of observation-to provide control of conditions and accuracy or permanence of recording.

6. Sponsorship and Administrative Cooperation

It is a common practice for the thesis to be sponsored by a faculty adviser in whose area of specialization the problem lies.

7. Costs and Returns

The candidate must consider carefully his own financial resources in the light of such facilities and assistance as can be provided by the institution.

8. Time Factor

As a general rule the minimum amount of graduate work for the Master's degree is one year, and for the Doctor's degree three years. Historical, experimental case and longitudinal genetic studies frequently require more time than the several types of normative survey work.

Hildreth Hoke McAshan has proposed an objective guide for judging the merits of a Problem.

The following questions may be raised for this purpose.

1. Is the problem really important?
2. Is the problem interesting to others?
3. Is the chosen problem a real problem?
4. Does the problem display originality and creativeness?
5. Am I really concerned with finding the solution?
6. Am I able to state hypotheses from the problem in a testable form?
7. Will I learn something new from this problem?
8. Do I understand the relationship of this specific problem to the broader problem area?
9. Will be able to select a sample from which I can generalize to some population?
10. Will some other intelligent person be able to replicate the study?

11. Will my proposed data-gathering instruments actually give the Information which I want?
12. Is the study, including the application of its results, practical? The number of affirmative answers should be required for a suitable problem.

Formulation of a Research Problem

Formulation of research problem begins with the selection of research area and ends with formulation of final statement of research problem. While formulating a research problem, a researcher typically follows the following steps –

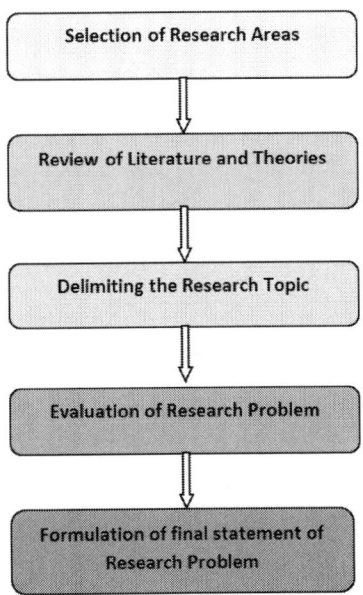

Steps in Formulation of a Research Problem

Selection of Research Area

Formulation of a research problem begins with selection of a broad research topic from personal experiences, literature, previous research & theories in which the researcher is interested and has significance for his profession.

Eg – Researcher gets an idea to conduct research on Innovations in Ethiopia, he or she initially begins with such broad research topic.

Review of Literature and Theories

After getting a broad idea for research he or she needs to review related literature and theories. Literature is reviewed to know what has already been done in this selected area of research. Reviewing of theories related to Innovation provides an opportunity for researcher to plan a research problem to contribute towards either testing or development of a theory/conceptual model.

De-Limiting the Research Topic

In this step the researcher proceeds from a general idea of interest to a more specific topic of research to conduct a study. Initially the researcher decides to conduct a research on 'Innovation in Ethiopia,' later in this stage he limits to 'Innovations in Construction Industry'

Evaluating the Research Problem

Once the researcher is clear about specific research problem, next the research problem must be carefully evaluated for its significance, research ability and feasibility. Feasibility of research problem should be evaluated for time, cost, availability of subjects and resources, administrative and peer support, Ethical considerations, researcher's competence and interests.

Formulating Final Statement of Research Problem

After establishing significance, researchablility and feasibility then the researcher finally formulates a final statement of research problem. A statement of research problem could be in declarative or interrogative form.

In a declarative format, a research problem is stated in declarative statement

Eg., "**A descriptive study** on factors affecting innovation trends in construction industry in Ethiopia" or "**An exploratory study** on contributing factors of sustainability of innovations in selected manufacturing companies in oromia region of Ethiopia"

In Interrogative format, a research problem is stated in question format. For example, "what is the influence of advertising on demand for a new model of automobile….. what is the effect of additional taxes on profitability and sustainability of an Industry" etc.…

The choice of either of these two types of format formulation of a research problem depends on the researchers preferences and institutional policies. However declarative format is much popular among academic researchers. For formulation of research problem, it is preferable if it fulfils the following criteria

- Research problem is clearly and precisely articulated
    - ✓ It clearly states the variables, population and research setting under study
    - ✓ Variables are expressed in measurable terms
    - ✓ The type of study may also be included in the statement of research problem.

For example in "**An exploratory study** on contributing factors of sustainability of innovations in selected manufacturing companies in oromia region of Ethiopia"

Research type – Exploratory research

Variables – factors of sustainability of innovations

Population – manufacturing companies in Oromia region

After formulating a research problem it is essential to write a research proposal

The Research Proposal

A research proposal or research synopsis or an outline of proposed works required by many universities and institutions, serves as a useful basis for the evaluation of a project as well as a guide line for the researcher. The synopsis contains a clear and concise statement of the problem, the hypothesis involved, a recognition of the significance of the problem, definitions of the important terms, assumptions and limitations, a resume of related literature, an analysis of proposed research producers, and a time schedule. This proposal or synopsis is placed before the research degree committee to examine its worth. The final approval is given by this committee at university level. It is like a blue print of research project.

The preparation of a research proposal or synopsis is an important step in the research process. A worthwhile research work is likely to result only from a well-prepared and well-designed proposal or research synopsis. A research proposal includes. the following essential parts:

1. The Problem and statement of the problem.
2. The Review of literature or theoretical framework of the study.
3. The Hypotheses and objectives.
4. The Methodology and procedure of the study.
5. Educational implications or significance of the problem.
6. Definitions, assumptions and delimitations.
7. A tentative structure of the report.
8. Bibliography.

1. The Statement of the Problem

This attempt to focus on a stated goal gives direction to the research process. It must be limited enough in scope to make a definite conclusion possible. A problem suggests a specific answer or conclusion. The statement of the problem should be written in specific clear-cut words.

The statement of problem may be first discussed in a broad way and finally come to a conclusive statement .

2. The Review of Related Literature

A brief summary of previous research should be given so that the researcher and reader may be familiar with what is already known and with what is still unknown and untested. The effective research is based upon past knowledge, this step helps to eliminate replication of what has been done and provides useful basis for the formulation of hypotheses and deciding the methodology of the study. A review of related literature should conclude with a comment of area of agreement and disagreement in findings.

3. The Hypotheses

A scientific study is based on hypotheses. It may be appropriate here to formulate a major hypotheses and several hypotheses. This approach clearly establishes the nature of the problem and the logic underlying the investigation. The hypothesis indicates the expected outcomes the investigation. The formulation of the hypotheses in advance of the data-gathering process is necessary for an unbiased investigation. The hypotheses should be first stated in positive or substantive form. In every investigation hypotheses can not be formulated but objectives of the study can be written to indicate the direction of the research work.

4. Methodology and Procedure of the Study

This part of the proposal outlines the entire research plan. Under this part of the synopsis method, sample, population, tools and statistical analysis techniques are described in view of testing the formulated hypotheses. It describes just what must be done, how it will be done, what data will be needed, what data-gathering devices will be employed, how sources of data will be selected, and how the data will be analyzed and conclusions be drawn.

5. Educational Implication or the Significance of the Problem

It is important part of research synopsis in which research points out the answer to the question or the solution to the problem may influence educational theory or practice. The implication of the finding of the study helps to give the project an urgency, justifying its worth. Social Studies Research study must have its implication to educational practices.

6. Definitions, Assumptions and Limitations

The statement of the problem or topic of the study includes some terms. These terms or variables should be defined clearly. At this stage operational definitions of terms are usually given in research proposal so that statement of the problem must convey the specific meaning. The variables of the study should be defined clearly and unambiguously in operational terms.

A study involves several variables which play different roles in the investigation. The role of the variable depends on the assumptions of the study. The sample of the study will be representative of the population. The assumptions of the study vary study to study. The feasibility of an investigation depends on the delimitations of the study. A study is delimited to its variables, sample, method, tools and statistical techniques of the study. These delimitations should be clearly mentioned in the synopsis of the study.

7. Structure of the Report

A tentative structure of the report is also written. It includes the list of chapters which will be included in the report of the thesis. These may be: Introductory or a theoretical framework. Review of literature, Methodology and procedure of the study. Data collection and Analysis of data, conclusions of the study.

8. Bibliography

The last part of the proposal provides the list of references in the form of bibliography which includes books of research, or conceptual framework, hand-books encyclopaedia, journals and unpublished and published thesis on the related area of the study. A proposal of research or synopsis is usually written in third person i.e. he or she or investigator, and in present or future tense. It is submitted to research degree committee's approval. This committee approves as it is or suggests some modifications or rejects the proposal. The researcher can begin only after the approval of the proposal by the committee.

Chapter 4

Literature review – Need, Objectives and Reporting

Review of Related Literature

The phrase 'review of literature' consists of two words: Review and Literature. The word 'literature' has conveyed different meaning from the traditional meaning. It is used with reference to the languages e.g. English literature,. It includes a subject content: prose, poetry, dramas, novels, stories etc. Here in research methodology the term literature refers to the knowledge of a particular area of investigation of any discipline which includes theoretical, practical and its research studies.

The term 'review' means to organize the knowledge of the specific area of research to evolve an edifice of knowledge to show that his study would be an addition to this field. The task of review of literature is highly creative and tedious because researcher has to synthesize the available knowledge of the field in a unique way to provide the rationale for his study.

The very words 'review' and 'literature' have quite different meanings in the historical approach. In historical research, the researcher does much more than review already published material, he seeks to discover and to integrate new information which has never been reported and never considered.

The concept and process implied in the term 'review of literature' have such different meanings in historical as compared with survey and experimental research.

Reviewing the literature has two phases. The first phase includes identifying all the relevant published material in the problem area and reading that part of it with which we are not thoroughly familiar. We develop the foundation of ideas and results on which our own study will be built. The second phase of the review of literature involves writing this foundation of ideas into a section of the research report. This section is for the joint benefit of the researchers and readers. For the researcher, it establishes the background in the field. For the readers it provides a summary of the thinking and research necessary for them to understand the study.

Need for Review of Literature

The review of literature is essential due to the following reasons:

1. One of the early steps in planning a research work is to review research done previously in the particular area of interest and relevant area quantitative and qualitative analysis of this research usually gives the worker an indication of the direction.

2. It is very essential for every investigator to be up-to-date in his information about the literature, related to his own problem already done by others. It is considered the most important prerequisite to actual planning and conducting the study.

3. It avoids the replication of the study of findings to take an advantage from similar or related literature as regards, to methodology, techniques of data collection, procedure adopted and conclusions drawn. He can justify his own endeavour in the field.

4. It provides as source of problem of study, an analogy may be drawn for identifying and selecting his own problem of research. The researcher formulates his hypothesis on the basis of review of literature. It also provides the rationale for the study. The results and findings of the study can also be discussed at length.

The review of literature indicates the clear picture of the problem to be solved. The scholarship in the field can be developed by reviewing the literature of the field.

Objectives of Review of Literature

The review of literature serves the following purposes in conducting research work:

1. It provides theories, ideas, explanations or hypothesis which may prove useful in the formulation of a new problem.
2. It indicates whether the evidence already available solves the problem adequately without requiring further investigation. It avoids the replication.
3. It provides the sources for hypothesis. The researcher can formulate research hypothesis on the basis of available studies.
4. It suggests method, procedure, sources of data and statistical techniques appropriate to the solution of the problem.
5. It locates comparative data and findings useful in the interpretation and discussion of results. The conclusions drawn in the related studies may be significantly compared and may be used as the subject for the findings of the study.
6. It helps in developing experts and general scholarship of the investigator in the area investigated.
7. It contributes towards the accurate knowledge of the evidence or literature in one's area of activity is a good avenue towards making oneself. This knowledge is an asset ever afterwards, whether one is employed in an institution of higher learning or a research organization.

Principles and Procedures for Review of Literature

The following is the specific procedure through which review can be done appropriately:

1. It is generally advisable to get first and over all view by consulting a general source, such as a text-book which is more likely to provide the meaning and nature of the concepts and variables or theoretical framework of the field. The logical starting point is to get a clear picture of the problem to be solved. A text-book usually provides

the theoretical aspects of the problem. It is very essential to develop deep understanding about the variables and the field.

2. After developing the insight about the general nature of his problem, the investigator should review the empirical researches of the area.. The researcher's major concern at this point should be to get a clear picture of the field as a whole; specific details are important at this stage. He should start from a topical outline and a temperature set of classifications, so that whatever he reads can be made meaningful.

3. The research for library material must be systematic and thorough. The investigator generally should start by collecting his references from the educational index. When a large number of references are to be copied, they should be typed because precision is required here.

4. The researcher should take note systematically in the light of such criteria as uniformity, accuracy and ease of assembly. The notes should be taken on the card. Each entry should be made separately; references should be recorded with complete bibliographic data. It should be recorded on front side of the card and content should be taken below and reverse side of it. Each note should be recorded carefully and accurately.

5. The investigator should take as complete notes as he might need. On the other hand, taking unnecessary notes is wasteful. The useful and necessary material should be recorded precisely. It would be better that similar sources are gathered. It is necessary that a general education of each source, rather than simply a summary of its content be made. Such evaluation is necessary both in presenting the study in the review of literature, and in using the study as background for the interpretation of the findings of the study.

6. A major pre-requisite for effective library work is the ability to read at high speed. This can only be developed through practice. He must learn to skim material to see what it has to contribute to the study, only after its reference has been established, it should be read in detail. Surveying the literature for the purpose of conducting research is not just 'a pleasant excursion in the wonderful word

of books,' it is a precise and exacting task of locating specific information for the specific purpose.

7. The actual note-taking process is always a difficult task for the researcher. He has to spend long hours in the library taking notes by hand. It is a very tedious job and leads to importance to carelessness and illegibility. He should make use of the facilities available in the library for this purpose.

Sources of Review of Literature

There are various sources of literature which may be used for this purpose. These sources can be broadly classified into these heads.

(1) Books and Text – Books material.

(2) The Periodical/Journals – A periodical is defined as a publication issued in successive parts, usually at regular intervals, and as a rule, intended to be continued indefinitely.

(3) Abstracts – Another type of reference guide is the abstract, review, or digest that usually give brief summaries of research studies.

(4) Dissertations and Theses – The theses and dissertations which embody the bulk of presenting educational research, are usually housed by the institutions and universities that award the authors their advanced degrees. Sometimes these studies are published in whole or in part in educational journals. The related dissertations and theses are the main sources of review of literature. the entry 'dissertations and theses' issue of the bibliographic index in the most comprehensive listing of sources to these research in progress.

Reporting Review of Literature

Generally review of literature is reported in the second chapter of the thesis or dissertation. The purpose of reporting the review of literature is not to write down research abstracts one by one which is usual practice of the researcher of to-day. It is most difficult and creative job on the part of researcher. The following procedure should be followed in reporting it :

1. The research should go through collected research studies of the field. He should make an attempt to exhaust all sources of review

of literature. He should try to evolve a criterion for classifying the studies. The usual or traditional classification is: studies conducted abroad and studies conducted in Ethiopia in your area of research.

2. After evolving criterion of classification, these studies, are arranged according to criterion. One type studies review should be reported separately. The similar type of findings should be given in next para, and he should try to relate with to his own study. This procedure should be followed for reporting all types of studies.

3. At the end of review of literature. he should try to summarize in brief to provide a global picture of whole knowledge of the studies. After that he should relate his study to them and evolve gaps. In the end he should show that his study is a derivation from these studies.

Suggestions for Reporting Review of Literature

The reviewing of literature is the continuous process. A researcher begins the review of literature even before selecting his problem of research. The review of literature generally helps in identifying and selecting a research problem. If researcher has selected a problem of his own or suggested by some expert; even then he has to review literature for its justification that it is a novel problem. After selecting and defining a problem, he has to formulate hypotheses for the problem. The review of literature provides the rationale or basis for these hypotheses. The rationale for method, sample tools and statistical technique are obtained from the review of the studies. The results and findings are discussed at length with the help of review of literature. The findings of earlier studies may support his formulation or contradict. He has to advance some reasons for it. The review of literature is used from selecting a problem upto reporting the findings of a study.

Second suggestion is that knowledge is increasing or advancing rapidly and research studies are on going process. A research scholar should remain in touch with library literature or the field throughout the period of his research work. He should be upto-date at the time of reporting review of literature and discussing his findings. The reporting review of literature makes the research study very scientific and up-to-data. It is not only useful in preparing and writing a thesis but mastery of the review of literature develops the scholarship in the researcher. He justifies in any interviews, seminars, conferences and also in his teaching job and professional growth.

Chapter 5

Research Design

Decisions regarding what, where, when, how much, by what means concerning an inquiry or a research study constitute a research design. "A research design is the arrangement of conditions for collection and analysis of data in a manner that aims to combine relevance to the research purpose with economy in procedure." In fact, the research design is the conceptual structure within which research is conducted; it constitutes the blueprint for the collection, measurement and analysis of data. As such the design includes an outline of what the researcher will do from writing the hypothesis and its operational implications to the final analysis of data. In short it is a framework or blue print for conducting research.

Parts of Research Design

(a) *The sampling design* which deals with the method of selecting items to be observed for the given study;

(b) *The observational design* which relates to the conditions under which the observations are to be made;

(c) *The statistical design* which concerns with the question of how many items are to be observed and how the information and data gathered are to be analyzed; and

(d) *The operational design* which deals with the techniques by which the procedures specified in the sampling, statistical and observational designs can be carried out.

Types of Research Design

Action Research Design – The essentials of action research design follow a characteristic cycle whereby initially an exploratory stance is adopted, where an understanding of a problem is developed and plans are made for some form of interventionary strategy. Then the intervention is carried out (the "action" in Action Research) during which time, pertinent observations are collected in various forms. The new interventional strategies are carried out, and this cyclic process repeats, continuing until a sufficient understanding of (or a valid implementation solution for) the problem is achieved. The protocol is iterative or cyclical in nature and is intended to foster deeper understanding of a given situation, starting with conceptualizing and particularizing the problem and moving through several interventions and evaluations.

Case Study Design – A case study is an in-depth study of a particular research problem rather than a sweeping statistical survey or comprehesive comparative inquiry. It is often used to narrow down a very broad field of research into one or a few easily researchable examples. The case study research design is also useful for testing whether a specific theory and model actually applies to phenomena in the real world. It is a useful design when not much is known about an issue or phenomenon.

Causal Design – Causality studies may be thought of as understanding a phenomenon in terms of conditional statements in the form, "If X, then Y." This type of research is used to measure what impact a specific change will have on existing norms and assumptions. Most social scientists seek causal explanations that reflect tests of hypotheses. Causal effect (nomothetic perspective) occurs when variation in one phenomenon, an independent variable, leads to or results, on average, in variation in another phenomenon, the dependent variable.

Cohort Design – Often used in the medical sciences, but also found in the applied social sciences, a cohort study generally refers to a study conducted over a period of time involving members of a population which the subject or representative member comes from, and who are united by some commonality or similarity. Using a quantitative framework, a cohort study makes note of statistical occurrence within a specialized subgroup, united by same or similar characteristics that are relevant to the research problem being investigated, rather than studying statistical occurrence within the general population. Using a qualitative framework, cohort studies generally gather data using methods of observation. Cohorts can be either "open" or "closed."

Open Cohort Studies [dynamic populations, such as the population of Los Angeles] involve a population that is defined just by the state of being a part of the study in question (and being monitored for the outcome). Date of entry and exit from the study is individually defined, therefore, the size of the study population is not constant. In open cohort studies, researchers can only calculate rate based data, such as, incidence rates and variants thereof.

Closed Cohort Studies [static populations, such as patients entered into a clinical trial] involve participants who enter into the study at one defining point in time and where it is presumed that no new participants can enter the cohort. Given this, the number of study participants remains constant (or can only decrease).

Cross-Sectional Design – Cross-sectional research designs have three distinctive features: no time dimension; a reliance on existing differences rather than change following intervention; and, groups are selected based on existing differences rather than random allocation. The cross-sectional design can only measure differences between or from among a variety of people, subjects, or phenomena rather than a process of change. As such, researchers using this design can only employ a relatively passive approach to making causal inferences based on findings.

Descriptive Design – Descriptive research designs help provide answers to the questions of who, what, when, where, and how associated with a particular research problem; a descriptive study cannot conclusively ascertain answers to why. Descriptive research is used to obtain information concerning the current status of the phenomena and to describe "what exists" with respect to variables or conditions in a situation.

Experimental Design – A blueprint of the procedure that enables the researcher to maintain control over all factors that may affect the result of an experiment. In doing this, the researcher attempts to determine or predict what may occur. Experimental research is often used where there is time priority in a causal relationship (cause precedes effect), there is consistency in a causal relationship (a cause will always lead to the same effect), and the magnitude of the correlation is great. The classic experimental design specifies an experimental group and a control group. The independent variable is administered to the experimental group and not to the control group, and both groups are measured on the same dependent variable. Subsequent experimental designs have used more groups and more measurements over longer periods. True experiments must have control, randomization, and manipulation.

Exploratory Design – An exploratory design is conducted about a research problem when there are few or no earlier studies to refer to or rely upon to predict an outcome. The focus is on gaining insights and familiarity for later investigation or undertaken when research problems are in a preliminary stage of investigation. Exploratory designs are often used to establish an understanding of how best to proceed in studying an issue or what methodology would effectively apply to gathering information about the issue.

Historical Design – The purpose of a historical research design is to collect, verify, and synthesize evidence from the past to establish facts that defend or refute a hypothesis. It uses secondary sources and a variety of primary documentary evidence, such as, diaries, official records, reports, archives, and non-textual information [maps, pictures, audio and visual recordings]. The limitation is that the sources must be both authentic and valid.

Longitudinal Design – A longitudinal study follows the same sample over time and makes repeated observations. For example, with longitudinal surveys, the same group of people is interviewed at regular intervals, enabling researchers to track changes over time and to relate them to variables that might explain why the changes occur. Longitudinal research designs describe patterns of change and help establish the direction and magnitude of causal relationships. Measurements are taken on each variable over two or more distinct time periods. This allows the researcher to measure change in variables over time. It is a type of observational study sometimes referred to as a panel study.

Meta-Analysis Design – Meta-analysis is an analytical methodology designed to systematically evaluate and summarize the results from a number of individual studies, thereby, increasing the overall sample size and the ability of the researcher to study effects of interest. The purpose is to not simply summarize existing knowledge, but to develop a new understanding of a research problem using synoptic reasoning. The main objectives of meta-analysis include analyzing differences in the results among studies and increasing the precision by which effects are estimated. A well-designed meta-analysis depends upon strict adherence to the criteria used for selecting studies and the availability of information in each study to properly analyze their findings. Lack of information can severely limit the type of analyzes and conclusions that can be reached. In addition, the more dissimilarity there is in the results among individual studies [heterogeneity], the more difficult it is to justify interpretations that govern a valid synopsis of results.

Mixed-Method Design – Mixed methods research represents more of an approach to examining a research problem than a methodology. Mixed method is characterized by a focus on research problems that require, 1) an examination of real-life contextual understandings, multi-level perspectives, and cultural influences; 2) an intentional application of rigorous quantitative research assessing magnitude and frequency of constructs and rigorous qualitative research exploring the meaning and understanding of the constructs; and, 3) an objective of drawing on the strengths of quantitative and qualitative data gathering techniques to formulate a holistic interpretive framework for generating possible solutions or new understandings of the problem. Tashakkori and Creswell (2007) and other proponents of mixed methods argue that the design encompasses more than simply combining qualitative and quantitative methods but, rather, reflects a new "third way" epistemological paradigm that occupies the conceptual space between positivism and interpretivism.

Features of a Good Research Design

Research design has to suit the requirement of your research. Therefore different studies require different research designs. However there are certain features of a good research design. A good research design is one that is flexible, appropriate, efficient and economical. Research design must minimize biases and maximize reliability of data collected and analyzed.

A good research design should satisfy the following four conditions namely objectivity, reliability, validity and generalization of the findings.

Objectivity – Objectivity refers to the findings related to the method of data collection and scoring of the responses. The research design should permit the measuring instrument which are fairly objective in which every observer scoring the performance must precisely give the same report. That is the objectivity of the procedure can be judged by the degree of agreement between the final scores assigned to different individuals by more than one independent observer. This ensures objectivity of data collected and capability of analysis and drawing generalizations.

Reliability – Reliability refers to consistency through out a series of measurements which means that if a respondent gives a particular reply to a question, he is expected to give the same answer even if he is asked repeatedly. Therefore the researcher should frame the items in a questionnaire in such a way that it provides consistency or reliability.

Validity – A measuring instrument is said to be valid when it measures what it is expected to measure. Example a test conducted to measure Perception must measure perception only and questions must be framed to meet this objective.

Generalization – This means that the data collected through a sample must be suitable for drawing conclusions about the population. A research design helps an investigator to generalize his findings for population. A good research design is capable of drawing such conclusions.

Categorizing Research Designs

In order to have a more clear understanding of how to design research, it is suitable to categorize them onto three major categories –

 a. Research design for Exploratory studies
 b. Research design for Descriptive and Diagnostic studies and,
 c. Research design for Experimental studies (Hypothesis testing)

Research Design for Exploratory studies – Exploratory research is a research conducted for a problem that has not been studied more clearly, establishes priorities and develops operational definitions. Such studies are also called as formulative research studies. The major emphasis in such studies is on discovery of new ideas and insights. Exploratory research may also be used in cases where you must define the problem more precisely, identify the necessary course of action and gain new insights before going on to confirm findings. Exploratory research design is meaningful in any situation where the researcher does not have enough understanding to proceed with project. Therefore exploratory research is characterized by flexibility with respect to methods. The primary characteristic of exploratory research design is that the overall design is flexible and mostly non – probability sampling method is used.

Parts of an Exploratory research design are –

Sampling Design – Non probability sampling design is used (eg. Purposive or judgemental sampling methods)

Statistical Design – There is no preplanned design for analysis

Observational Design – Unstructured instruments are used for collection of data

Operational Design – There is no fixed or predetermined decision about operational procedures.

Therefore, exploratory research designs have an overall flexible structure.

Exploratory research designs are mostly used –

To obtain background information especially when nothing is known about the problem area.

There is a need to define problem areas and formulate hypothesis for further investigation.

To explore and identify new concepts

Reduce a large number of possible projects to a small number of probable ones.

To identify behaviourial patterns, beliefs, attitudes motivations etc.

To identify and explore reasons that lie behind the statistical differences between groups that emerged in secondary data or surveys.

When exploring sensitive and personally embarrassing issues from respondents.

When there are issues that are difficult for the respondents to rationalize and articulate easily.

To identify hitherto unknown connections between different measured variables.

Research design for descriptive and diagnostic studies - Descriptive research studies are those studies that are concerned with describing the characteristics of a particular individual or a group. Diagnostic research studies on the other hand determine the frequency with which something occurs or its association with something else. Most of social sciences research is descriptive in nature. Descriptive and diagnostic research designs have certain common characteristics. In both descriptive and diagnostic research designs, the researcher must be able to define the relevant population for the study. The overall research design therefore is rigid and not flexible.

Sampling Design – Probability sampling design is used (eg. Random sampling method)

Statistical Design – There is preplanned design for analysis

Observational Design – Structured instruments are used for collection of data

Operational Design – Predetermined or advanced decision about operational procedures.

Therefore, Descriptive and diagnostic research designs have an overall rigid structure.

Research design for Experimental studies (Hypothesis testing) – Experimental studies (also known as hypothesis testing studies) are those studies where the researcher experiments and tests hypothesis in order to establish relationship between identified variables. Experimental research designs may be further categorized as 'Formal' and 'Informal' experimental designs. Informal experimental designs are those that normally use a less sophisticated form of analysis. Formal experimental designs offer relatively more control and use precise statistical procedures for analysis. Informal and formal research designs will be discussed separately in the following sections.

Informal Experimental Research Designs – Basically there are three types of informal experimental research designs. These are

Before and after – with out control design

Before and after – with control design

After only – with control design

In Before and after – with out control design, a single group or area is selected and the dependent variable is measured before the introduction of the treatment. The treatment is then introduced and the dependent variable is measured again after the treatment has been introduced. Thus the effect of the treatment is measured as a difference in the phenomenon before and after the treatment. The main difficulty faced in such a design is that with passage of time, there may be certain extraneous factors that effect treatment.

In after only – with control designs, two groups or areas are selected and the treatment is introduced into the test area only. The dependent variable is measured in both areas at the same time. The treatment impact is measured by subtracting the value of the dependent variable in the control area from its value in the test area. The primary assumption is such a design is that the two areas are similar with respect to their behavior towards the phenomenon considered, if this assumption is not true then there is a possibility of extraneous variation entering into the treatment effect. However since the measurement is done in the same time period, the possibility of time impact is eliminated.

In Before and after – with control designs, two areas are selected and the dependent variable is measured in both the areas for an identical time period before the treatment. The treatment is then introduced into the test area only and the dependent variable is measured in both for an identical time period after the introduction of the treatment. The effect of the treatment is determined by subtracting the change in the dependent variable in the control area from the change in the dependent variable in test area.

Formal Experimental Research Designs can be categorized into Completely randomized designs, Randomized block design, Latin square design and Factorial design (Kothari, 2004)

Completely randomized designs – This is the simplest possible design and the procedures are also simple. The main characteristic of such design is that subjects are randomly assigned to experimental treatments. For example if there are 100 subjects and we want to test 50 subjects under treatment procedure A and 50 under treatment procedure B, then there is every possibility that group of 50 selected from a set of 100 subjects have an equal opportunity of being assigned to treatment A and treatment B (one –way anova is used to analyze such a design)

Randomized block design – this is an improvement over the Completely Randomised design. In this design subjects are first divided into groups or known blocks such that each groups subjects are relatively similar with respect to some selected variable. Blocks are levels at which we hold the extraneous factor fixed so that its contribution to the total variability of data can be measured, Random block designs are analyzed by two way ANOVA technique.

In Latin Square Design – This design is often used in agricultural research as the conditions under which agricultural research is carried out is quiet different from other types of research. The latin square design is used where the researcher desires to control the variation in an experiment that is related to rows and columns in the field. Treatmetns are assigned at random within rows and columns with each treatment once per row and once per column.

The latin square design gets its name from the fact that we can write it as a square with latin letters to correspond to the treatments. The treatment factor levels are the latin letters in the latin square design. The number of rows and columns has to correspond to the number of treatment levels. If we have four treatments then we would need to have four rows and four columns in order to create a latin square. This gives us a design where we have each of the treatments and in each row and in each column.

Factorial Designs – These designs are used in experiments where the effects of varying more than one factor are to be determined. These are used in economic and social conditions where a large number of factors affect a particular problem. Factorial designs are of two types – simple factorial designs and complex factorial designs.

In a simple factorial design, the effects of varying two factors on a dependent variable is considered. These are also called as 'two factor factorial design.' In complex factorial designs more than two factors are considered. These are known as 'multifactor factorial design.'

Simple factorial design may be either a 2×2 or 3×4 or 5×3 type. Incase of a complex factoial design with three factors with one experimental variable having two treatments and two control variables, each one of which having two levels, the design will be termed as 2×2×2 complex factorial design that contains a total of eight cells.

Chapter 6
Hypothesis Designing

Hypothesis

Meaning of the word Hypothesis - The word hypothesis is made up of two Greek roots which mean that it is some sort of 'sub-statements,' for it is the presumptive statement of a proposition, which the investigation seeks to prove. The scientist observes the man of special class of phenomena and broods over it until by a flash of insight he perceives an order and intelligent harmony in it. This is often referred to as an 'explanation' of the facts he has observed. He has a 'theory' about particular mass of fact. This theory when stated as a testable proposition formally and clearly subjected to empirical or experimental verification is known as a hypothesis. Hypothesis therefore, is a question that the researcher formally defines and either proves or disproves.

The word hypothesis consists of two words:

Hypo + thesis = Hypothesis

'Hypo' means tentative or subject to the verification and 'Thesis' means statement about solution of a problem.

The general meaning of the term hypothesis is a tentative statement about the solution of the problem. Hypothesis offers a solution of the problem that is to be verified empirically and based on some rationale.

Another meaning of the word hypothesis which is composed of two words:

'Hypo' means composition of two or more variables which is to be verified.

'Thesis' means position of these variables in the specific frame of reference.

This is the operational meaning of the term hypothesis. Hypothesis is the composition of some variables which have some specific position or role of the variables i.e. to be verified empirically. It is a proposition about the factual and conceptual' elements.

A tentative generalization or theory formulated about the character of phenomena under observation are called hypothesis. It is a statement temporarily accepted as in the light of what is known at the time about the phenomena. It is the basis for planning and action- in the research for new truth.

From a general point of view, when one talks about hypothesis, one simply means a mere assumption or some supposition to be proved or disproved. But for a researcher hypothesis is a formal question that he intends to resolve. Thus a hypothesis may be defined as a proposition or a set of proposition set forth as an explanation for the occurrence of some specified group of phenomena either asserted merely as a provisional conjecture to guide some investigation or accepted as highly probable in the light of established facts. Quite often a research hypothesis is a predictive statement, capable of being tested by scientific methods, that relates an independent variable to some dependent variable.

For example, consider statements like the following ones:

Employees who received training performed better

Performance of group A is same as that of group B etc.

Some Definitions of the Term Hypothesis

- A tentative supposition or provisional guess "It is a tentative supposition or provisional guess which seems to explain the situation under observation." – *James E. Greighton*
- A Tentative generalization- A Lungberg thinks "A hypothesis is a tentative generalisation the validity of which remains to be tested. In its most elementary stage the hypothesis may be any hunch, guess, imaginative idea which becomes the basis for further investigation."

- According to John W. Best, "It is a shrewd guess or inference that is formulated and provisionally adopted to explain observed facts or conditions and to guide in further investigation."
- According to A.D. Carmichael, "Science employs hypothesis in guiding the thinking process. When our experience tells us that a given phenomenon follows regularly upon the appearance of certain other phenomena, we conclude that the former is connected with the latter by some sort of relationship and we form an hypothesis concerning this relationship."
- A proposition is to be put to test to determine its validity: Goode and Han, "A hypothesis states what we are looking for. A hypothesis looks forward. It is a proposition which can be put to a test to determine its validity. It may prove to be correct or incorrect."
- An expectation about events based on generalization: Bruce W. Tuckman, "A hypothesis then could be defined as an expectation about events based on generalization of the assumed relationship between variables."

Nature of Hypothesis

The following are the main features of a hypothesis that explain its nature:

- It is conceptual in nature. Some kind of conceptual elements in the framework are involved in a hypothesis.
- It is a verbal statement in a declarative form. It is a verbal expression of ideas and concepts, it is not merely idea but in the verbal form, the idea is ready enough for empirical verification.
- It has the empirical referent. A hypothesis contains some empirical referent. It indicates the tentative relationship between two or more variables.
- It has a forward or future reference. A hypothesis is future oriented. It relates to the future verification not the past facts and information.
- It is the pivot of a scientific research. All the research activities are designed for its verification.

The nature of hypothesis can be well understood when we differentiate it with other terms like assumption and postulate.

Assumption means taking things for granted so that the situation is simplified for logical procedure. For example, the formulas of Statistics and measurement are based on number of assumptions. Assumption means restrictive conditions before the argument can become valid.

Postulates are the working beliefs of most scientific activity. The mathematician begins by postulating a system of numbers which range from 0 to 9 and can permute and combine only thereafter.

Where as, A **hypothesis** is different from both of these. It is the presumptive statement of a proposition which the investigator seeks to prove. It is a condensed generalization. This generalization requires a knowledge of principles of things or essential characteristics which pertain to entire class of phenomena.

Some Basis Characteristics of a Hypothesis

Hypothesis must possess the following characteristics:

i. Hypothesis should be clear and precise. If the hypothesis is not clear and precise, the inferences drawn on its basis cannot be taken as reliable.

ii. Hypothesis should be capable of being tested.. Some prior study may be done by researcher in order to make hypothesis a testable one. A hypothesis "is testable if other deductions can be made from it which, in turn, can be confirmed or disproved by observation."

iii. Hypothesis should state relationship between variables, if it happens to be a relational hypothesis.

iv. Hypothesis should be limited in scope and must be specific. A researcher must remember that narrower hypotheses are generally more testable and he should develop such hypotheses.

v. Hypothesis should be stated as far as possible in most simple terms so that the same is easily understandable by all concerned. But one must remember that simplicity of hypothesis has nothing to do with its significance.

vi. Hypothesis should be consistent with most known facts i.e., it must be consistent with a substantial body of established facts. In other words, it should be one which judges accept as being the most likely.

vii. Hypothesis should be amenable to testing within a reasonable time. One should not use even an excellent hypothesis, if the same cannot be tested in reasonable time for one cannot spend a life-time collecting data to test it.

viii. Hypothesis must explain the facts that gave rise to the need for explanation. This means that by using the hypothesis plus other known and accepted generalizations, one should be able to deduce the original problem condition. Thus hypothesis must actually explain what it claims to explain; it should have empirical reference.

Kinds of Hypothesis

Hypotheses vary in form and some extent, form is determined by some function. Thus a working hypothesis or a tentative hypothesis is described as the best guess or statement derivable from known or available evidence. The following kinds of hypotheses and their examples represent an attempt to order the more commonly observed varieties as well as to provide some general guidelines for hypothesis, development and statement.

There are four kinds of hypotheses: (*a*) Question (*b*) Declaration Statement (*c*) Directional Statement and (*d*) Null form or Non-Directional.

(*a*) **Question form of Hypotheses:** Some writers assert that a hypothesis may be stated as a question, however, there is no general consensus on this view. At best, it represents the simplest level of empirical observation. In fact, it fails to fit most definitions of hypothesis.

It is included here for two reasons: the first of which is simply that it frequently appears in the lists. The second reason is not so much that question may or may not qualify as a hypothesis. There are cases of simple investigation and search which can be adequately implemented by raising a question, rather than dichotomize hypothesis forms into acceptable/rejectable categories. The following example of a question is used to illustrate the various hypothesis forms:

Is there a significant interaction effect of schedule of reinforcement and extroversion on learning outcomes?

(b) **Declarative Statement:** A hypothesis may be developed as a declarative which provide an anticipated relationship or difference between variables. The anticipation of a difference between variables would imply that the hypothesis developer has examined existing evidence which led him to believe a difference may be anticipated as processes additional evidence.

The following is an example of this form of hypothesis-

H: There is significant interaction effect of schedule of reinforcement and extroversion on learning outcomes.

It is merely a declaration of the independent variables effect on the criterion variable.

(c) **Directional Hypothesis:** A hypothesis may be directional which connotes an expected direction in the relationship or difference between variables. The above hypothesis has been written in directional statement form as follows:

H: Extrovert learns better through intermittent schedule of reinforcement whereas introvert learns through continuous schedule of reinforcement.

The hypothesis developer of this type appears more certain of his anticipated evidence than would be the case if he had used either of the previous examples. If seeking a tenable hypothesis is the general interest of the researcher, this kind of hypothesis is less safe than the others because it reveals two possible conditions. These conditions are matter of degree. The first condition is that the problem of seeking relationship between variables is so obvious that additional evidence is scarcely needed. The second condition derives because researcher has examined the variables very thoroughly and the available evidence supports the statement of a particular anticipated outcomes.

An example of the obviously safe hypothesis would be 'hypothesis' that high intelligence students learn better than low intelligent students. The above hypothesis is in the directional statement form but it requires evidence for the relationship of these two variables reinforcement and personality.

(*d*) **Non-Directional Hypothesis:** A hypothesis may be stated in the null form which is an assertion that no relationship or no difference exists between or among the variables. This form null hypothesis is a statistical hypothesis which is testable within the framework of probability theory. It is also a non- directional form of hypothesis. The following are the examples of null form of hypothesis

$H0$: There is no significant interaction effect of schedule of reinforcement and extroversion on learning outcomes.

$H0$: There is no significant relationship between intelligence and achievement of students.

Variables in a Hypothesis

A hypothesis is made testable by providing operational definitions for the terms or variables of the hypothesis. For a testable hypothesis there are two important things :

1. Variables, and
2. Operational definitions.

Variables – There are five types of variables.

(*i*) Independent variable

(*ii*) Dependent variable

(*iii*) Moderator variable

(*iv*) Control variable

(*v*) Intervening variable

Let us consider a research among students of the same age and intelligence for measuring, skill performance as related to the number of practice traits particularly among boys but less directly among girls. Then the hypothesis for this condition would direct towards.

'Among students of the same age and intelligence, **skill performance is directly related to the number of practice traits** particularly among boys but less directly among girls'

In such a hypothesis the variables which must be considered are:

(*i*) Independent variable – number of practice trails.

(*ii*) Dependent variable – skill performance.

(*iii*) Moderator variable – sex.

(*iv*) Control variable – age, intelligence.

(*v*) Intervening variable – learning.

(*i*) The Independent Variable: The independent variable which is a stimulus variable or input operates either within a person or within environment to affect his behaviour. It is that factor which is measured, manipulated. or selected by the experimenter to determine its relationship to an observed phenomena.

If a researcher is studying the relationship between two variables X and Y. If X is independent variable, then it affects another variable Y: So the characteristics of independent variables are:

(*a*) It is the cause for change in other variables.

(*b*) Independent variables are always interested only it affects another variable, not in what affects it.

(*ii*) The Dependent Variable: The dependent variable is response variable or output. It is an observed aspect of the behaviour of an organism that has been stimulated. The dependent variable is that factor which is observed and measured to determine the effect of the independent variables. It is the variable that will change as a result of variations in the independent variable. It is considered dependent because its value depends upon the value of the independent variable. It represents the consequence of change in the parson or situation studied.

Relationship Between Independent and Dependent Variables: Most experiments involve many variables when two continuous variables are compared, as in correlation studies, deciding which variable to call independent and which dependent is sometimes arbitrary. In such cases variables are often not labelled as independent or dependent since there is no real distinction. Independent variables may be called factor and their variation may be called levels.

(iii) The Moderator Variable: The term moderator variable describes a special type of independent variable a secondary independent variable selected for study to determine if it affects the relationship between the primary independent variable and the dependent variable.

The moderator variable is defined as that factor which is measured, manipulated or selected by the experimenter to discover whether it modifies the relationship of independent variable to an observed phenomena. The sex and rural urban generally function as moderator variables.

(iv) Control Variable: All the variables in a situation can not be studied at the same time, some must be neutralized to guarantee that they will not have a differential or moderating effect on the relationship between the independent and dependent variables. These variables whose effects must be neutralized or controlled are known as control variables. They are defined as those factors which are controlled by experimenter to cancel out or neutralize any effect they might otherwise have on the observed phenomena. **While the effects of the control variables are neutralized, the effect of moderator variables are studied.**

Certain variables appear repeatedly as control variables, although they occasionally serve as moderator variables. For example sex, intelligence and socio-economic status are three subject variables that are commonly controlled, noise, task order and task content are common control variables in the situation.

(v) Intervening Variable: Each independent, moderator, and control variable can be manipulated by the experimenter and each variation can be observed by him as it affects the dependent variable. Often these variables are not concrete but hypothetical, the relationship between a hypothetical underlying or intervening variable and dependent variable.

An intervening variable is that factor which affects the observed phenomenon but cannot be seen and measured or manipulated, Its effect must be inferred from the effects of the Independent and moderator variables on the observed phenomena. The attitude, learning process, habit and interest function as Intervening variables.

After selecting the independent and dependent variables the researcher must decide which variables are to be included as moderator variables and which are to be excluded or hold constant as Control variables.

He must decide how to treat the total part of the other variables (other than the independent). That might effect the dependent variables. In making these decisions which variables are 'in' and which are 'out' he should take into account three kinds of considerations:

1. *Theoretical Consideration*: In treating as a moderator variable, the researcher learns how it interacts with the independent variable to produce differential effects on the dependent variable. In term of theoretical base researcher is working and in term of what he is trying to find out in a particular experiment, certain variables highly qualify as the moderator variables. In choosing a moderator variable a researcher should ask: Is the variable related to the theory with which I am working? How helpful would it be to know if an interaction exists? How likely is there to be an interaction?

2. *Design Consideration*: The questions which relate to the experimental design which has been chosen and its adequacy for controlling for sources of bias, the researcher should ask the following question: Have my decision about moderator and control variables met the requirements of experimental design in terms of dealing with the source of validity?

3. *Practical Consideration*: A researcher can only study so many variables at one time. There are limits to human and financial resources and the dead lines he can meet. By their nature some variables are harder to study than to neutralize, while others are as easily studied as neutralized.

The Research Variables Combined

The various research variables interact among themselves. The Independent, moderator, and control variables are under the researcher's control. They cause an impact within the subject. The impact is referred to as the intervening variable. In addition, the extraneous variables have an impact upon this Intervening variable. Such extraneous variables are not under the researcher's control, their presence weakens a study. One of the goals of a researcher is to remove as many significant factors as possible from the extraneous variables category by bringing them into the categories of moderator and control variables. Such a process of removing extraneous variables strengthens a study.

Variables in a Research Process

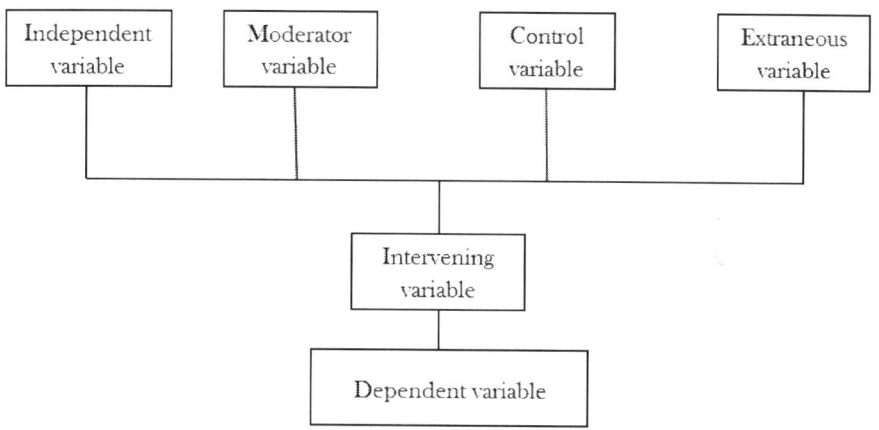

The intervening variable is merely hypothesized. It is abstract in nature. It cannot be visually observed. It is defined in conceptual terms. It is produced by some combination of the casual variables in the top row of the figure. It produces the effect or dependent variable.

Every experimental study has at least one independent variable and one dependent variable.

Both of these variables should be explicitly stated in the hypothesis and in the research predictor. If either the treatment or the outcome variable is too complex to be stated succinctly, further operational definitions of these variables can be included in the methods section of a report. Every study has also an intervening variable, and often there can be more than one intervening variable.

The intervening variable is, not stated in operational terms, but rattier conceptual explanation for the observed results. Intervening variables are normally not stated in the hypothesis or research prediction. Sometimes intervening variables are only vaguely described or are not mentioned at all.

Every study does not contain moderator and control variables. When such variables are contained in a study, they should be operationally defined. Moderator and control variables are stated in the research hypothesis and in the research prediction. Often the operational definitions further explanation in the method section of a report.

Eg: - Identify each of the research variable from the following hypothesis-

University engineering students who study management for two years will develop better accounting skills than those who do not study management.

Independent variable – studying management Vs not studying it.

Dependent variable – Better accounting skills

Moderator – Accounting skill level (advanced Vs. non – advanced)

Control – University engineering students

Intervening variable – Increased ability

Operational Definitions

Immediately upon completion of the testable hypotheses a researcher should examine them and the problem in general to determine if there are any terms which may be abstract or misleading. If he finds any such terns particularly in the testing hypotheses, they should be defined to make them completely operational for the study being undertaken.

The necessity for operational definitions does not mean that the researcher can define a term to mean whatever he cares to make it mean, but does enable the researcher to limit the meaning of a word. Operational definition should be more specific than those used in ordinary discourse. In other words any special term which must be used in the statement of the problem may require an operational definition to ensure clarity. Particular clarification should be given to terms which are used in the formulation of testable hypothesis. The term selected must be useful and make sense. Even common adjectives may be used if you adequately explain what you mean. A point to remember is that once a researcher makes a definition, he must stick to it.

Words which may need defining are those which appear ambiguous, which have confusing interpretation and which might make a difference to a person attempting to replicate the study.

An operational definition is a definition based on the observable characteristics of that which is being defined. The word 'observable' in the significant word in describing an operational definition. There are three approaches to constructing operational definitions:

Type A,

Type B, and

Type C.

Type 'A' Operational Definition: The 'Type A' operational definition can be constructed in terms of the operations that must be performed to cause the phenomenon or state than an object or thing. It tells what manipulation to use to induce a particular state. They are useful in defining independent variables as prescriptions carried out by the experimenter. The same variable, of course, be operationally defined by more than one type of definition but when what variable is the independent variable. It is often the most useful.

'Type B' Operational Definition: The 'Type B' operational definition can be constructed in terms of how the particular object or thing being defined operates, that is, what it does or what constitutes its dynamic properties. 'Type B' operational definitions see particularly appropriate in an educational context for describing a type of person. Though they may be used to define other variables, Type B definitions are particularly useful for defining the dependent variable when it is to be operationally based on behaviour.

'Type C' Operational Definitions: The 'Type C' operational definition can be constructed in terms of what the object or phenomenon being defined looks like, that is, what constitute its static properties. An Intelligent student can be defined as a person who has good memory, a large vocabulary, good reasoning ability, good arithmetic, skills etc. This type of operational definitions utilize observable structural properties of the object. It describes the qualities, traits, or characteristics of people or thing. Thus, they may be used for defining any type of variable when used for defining a person's characteristics, they specify the static or internal qualities rather than his behaviour as does the 'Type B' definition. 'Type C' operational definitions often lend themselves to measurement by tests although the ability to be tested is in requisite part of the definition.

The test ability of any hypothesis depends on whether suitable operational definitions can be constructed for its variables.

Chapter 7

Determining the Objects of Analysis

Research work is guided by inductive thinking. The researcher proceeds from specificity to generality. The sampling is the fundamental to all the statistical techniques and statistical analysis. The measures of a sample are known as statistics and measures of a population are termed as parameters. Mean, Standard deviation and Coefficient of Correlation of sample observations are known statistics and Mean S.D. and Coefficient of Correlation of a population are called parameters. Generally parameters are estimated on the basis of sample statistics. The accuracy of the parameters depends on sample representativeness or statistics. In research work generalization is made by estimating parameters on the basis of sample statistics.

Sample Design – A sample design is a definite plan for obtaining a sample from a given population. It refers to the technique or the procedure the researcher would adopt in selecting items for the sample. Sample design may as well lay down the number of items to be included in the sample i.e., the size of the sample. Sample design is determined before data are collected. There are many sample designs from which a researcher can choose. Some designs are relatively more precise and easier to apply than others. Researcher must select/prepare a sample design which should be reliable and appropriate for his research study.

Steps in Sample Design – While developing a sampling design, the researcher must pay attention to the following points:

(i) **Type of Universe:** The first step in developing any sample design is to clearly define the set of objects, technically called the Universe, to be studied. The universe can be finite or infinite. In finite universe the number of items is certain, but in case of an infinite universe the number of items is infinite, i.e., we cannot have any idea about the total number of items. The population of a city, the number of workers in a factory and the like are examples of finite universes, whereas the number of stars in the sky, listeners of a specific radio programme, etc. are examples of infinite universes.

(ii) **Sampling Unit:** A decision has to be taken concerning a sampling unit before selecting sample. Sampling unit may be a geographical one such as state, district, village, etc., or a construction unit such as house, flat, etc., or it may be a social unit such as family, club, school, etc., or it may be an individual. The researcher will have to decide one or more of such units that he has to select for his study.

(iii) **Sampling Frame/Source List:** It is also known as 'sampling frame' from which sample is to be drawn. It contains the names of all items of a universe (in case of finite universe only). If source list is not available, researcher has to prepare it. Such a list should be comprehensive, correct, reliable and appropriate. It is extremely important for the source list to be as representative of the population as possible.

(iv) **Size of Sample:** This refers to the number of items to be selected from the universe to constitute a sample. This a major problem before a researcher. The size of sample should neither be excessively large, nor too small. It should be optimum. An optimum sample is one which fulfills the requirements of efficiency, representativeness, reliability and flexibility. While deciding the size of sample, researcher must determine the desired precision as also an acceptable confidence level for the estimate.. The size of population must be kept in view for this also limits the sample size. The parameters of interest in a research study must be kept in view, while deciding the size of the sample. Costs too dictate the size of sample that we can draw. As such, budgetary constraint must invariably be taken into consideration when we decide the sample size.

(v) **Parameters of Interest:** In determining the sample design, one must consider the question of the specific population parameters which are of interest. For instance, we may be interested in estimating the proportion of persons with some characteristic in the population, or we may be interested in knowing some average or the other measure concerning the population. There may also be important sub-groups in the population about whom we would like to make estimates. All this has a strong impact upon the sample design we would accept.

(vi) **Budgetary Constraint:** Cost considerations, from practical point of view, have a major impact upon decisions relating to not only the size of the sample but also to the type of sample. This fact can even lead to the use of a non-probability sample.

(vii) **Sampling Procedure:** Finally, the researcher must decide the type of sample he will use i.e., he must decide about the technique to be used in selecting the items for the sample. In fact, this technique or procedure stands for the sample design itself. There are several sample designs (explained in the pages that follow) out of which the researcher must choose one for his study. Obviously, he must select that design which, for a given sample size and for a given cost, has a smaller sampling error.

Types of Techniques of Sampling

Several methods have been devised to select representative samples. In general two types of techniques of sampling are as follows:

1. **Probability Sampling:** Method of sampling which gives the probability that our sample is representative of population is known as probability sampling. Probability sampling is also known as 'random sampling' or 'chance sampling.' Under this sampling design, every item of the universe has an equal chance of inclusion in the sample.

2. **Non-probability Sampling** is also known as non-parametric sampling: Non-probability sampling is that sampling procedure which does not afford any basis for estimating the probability that each item in the population has of being included in the sample. Non-probability sampling is also known by different names such as deliberate sampling, purposive sampling and judgment sampling. In

this type of sampling, items for the sample are selected deliberately by the researcher; his choice concerning the items remains supreme. In other words, under non-probability sampling the organizers of the inquiry purposively choose the particular units of the universe for constituting a sample on the basis that the small mass that they so select out of a huge one will be typical or representative of the whole.

Characteristics of Probability Sampling

The following are the main characteristics of probability sampling:

1. In probability sampling we refer from the sample as well as the population.
2. In probability sampling every individual of the population has equal probability to be taken into the sample.
3. Probability sample may be representative of the population.
4. The observations (data) of the probability sample are used for the inferential purpose.
5. Probability sample has not from distribution for any variable.
6. Inferential or parametric statistics are used for probability sample.
7. There is a risk for drawing conclusions from probability sample.
8. The probability is comprehensive. Representativeness refers to characteristic. Comprehensiveness refers to size and area.

Characteristics of Non-Probability Sampling

The following are the main characteristics of non probability sample:

1. There is no idea of population in non-probability sampling.
2. There is no probability of selecting any individual.
3. Non-probability sample has free distribution.
4. The observations of non-probability sample are not used for generalization purpose.
5. Non-parametric or non-inferential statistics are used in non probability sample.

6. There is no risk for drawing conclusions from non-probability sample

Types or Techniques Probability Sampling: There are a number of techniques of taking probability sample.

But here only six important techniques have been discussed as follows:

1. Simple random sampling.
2. Systematic sampling.
3. Stratified sampling.
4. Multiple or Double sampling.
5. Multi-stage sampling.
6. Cluster sampling.

Types of Non-Probability Sample: There are the following four types of non-probability sample:

1. Incidental or accidental sample.
2. Purposive sample.
3. Quota sample.
4. Judgment sample.

Simple Random Sampling

A simple random sample is one in which each element of the population has an equal and independent chance of being included in the sample i.e. a sample selected by randomization method is known as simple-random sample and this technique is simple random-sampling.

Randomization is a method and is done by using a number of techniques as:

(a) Tossing a coin.
(b) Throwing a dice.
(c) Lottery method.
(d) Blind folded method.
(e) By using random table of 'Tippett's Table.'

Advantages

    (a) It requires a minimum knowledge of population.

    (b) It is free from subjectivity and free from personal error.

    (c) It provides appropriate data for our purpose.

    (d) The observations of the sample can be used for inferential purpose.

Disadvantages

    (a) The representativeness of a sample cannot be ensured by this method.

    (b) This method does not use the knowledge about the population.

    (c) The inferential accuracy of the finding depends upon the size of the sample

Systematic Sampling

Systematic sampling is an improvement over the simple random sampling. This method requires the complete information about the population. There should be a list of information of all the individuals of the population in any systematic way. Now we decide the size of the sample.

    Let sample size = n

    and population size = N

Now we select each N/n^{th} individual from the list and thus we have the desired size of sample which is known as systematic sample. Thus for this technique of sampling population should be arranged in any systematic way.

Advantages

    (a) This is a simple method of selecting a sample.

    (b) It reduces the field cost.

    (c) Inferential statistics may be used.

    (d) Sample may be comprehensive and representative of population.

    (e) Observations of the sample may be used for drawing conclusions and generalizations.

Disadvantages

(a) This is not free from error, since there is subjectivity due to different ways of systematic list by different individuals. Knowledge of population is essential.

(b) Information of each individual is essential.

(c) This method can't ensure the representativeness.

(d) There is a risk in drawing conclusions from the observations of the sample.

Stratified Sampling

It is an improvement over the earlier method. When employing this technique, the researcher divides his population in strata on the basis of some characteristics and from each of these smaller homogeneous groups (strata) draws at random a predetermined number of units. Researcher should choose that characteristic or criterion which seems to be more relevant in his research work.

Stratified sampling may be of three types:

1. Disproportionate stratified sampling.
2. Proportionate stratified sampling.
3. Optimum allocation stratified sampling.

    1. Disproportionate sampling means that the size of the sample in each unit is not proportionate to the size of the unit but depends upon considerations involving personal judgment and convenience. This method of sampling is more effective for comparing strata which have different error possibilities. It is less efficient for determining population characteristics.

    2. Proportionate sampling refers to the selection from each sampling unit of a sample that is proportionate to the size of the unit. Advantages of this procedure include representativeness with respect to variables used as the basis of classifying categories and increased chances of being able to make comparisons between strata. Lack of information on proportion of the population in each category and faulty classification may be listed as disadvantages of this method.

3. Optimum allocation stratified sampling is representative as well as comprehensive than other stratified samples. It refers to selecting units from each stratum should be in proportion to the corresponding stratum the population. Thus sample obtained is known as optimum allocation stratified sample.

Advantages

(a) It is (more precisely third way) a good representative of the population.

(b) It is an improvement over the earlier.

(c) It is an objective method of sampling.

(d) Observations can be used for inferential purpose.

Disadvantages

(a) Serious disadvantage of this method is that it is difficult for the researcher to decide the relevant criterion for stratification.

(b) Only one criterion can be used for stratification, but it generally seems more than one criterion relevant for stratification.

(c) It is costly and time consuming method.

(d) Selected sample may be representative with reference to the used criterion but not for the other.

(e) There is a risk in generalization

Multiple or Double or Repetitive Sampling

Generally this is not a new method but only a new application of the samplings we discussed above. This is most frequently used for establishing the reliability of a sample. When employing a mailed questionnaire, double sampling is sometimes used to obtain a 'more representative sample. This is done because some randomly selected subjects who are sent questionnaires may not return them. Obviously, the missing data will bias the result of the study, if the people who fail to reply the' query differ in some fundamental way from the others in respect to the phenomena being studied. To eliminate this bias, a second sample may be drawn at random from the non-respondents and the people interviewed to obtain the desired information. Thus this technique is also known as repeated or multiple sampling.

This double sampling technique enables one to check on the reliability of the information obtained from the first sample. Thus, double sampling, wherein one sample is analysed, and information obtained is used to draw the next sample to examine the problem further.

Advantages

(a) This sampling procedure leads to the inferences of free determine precision based on a number of observations.

(b) This technique of sampling reduces the error.

(c) This method maintains the procedure of the finding evaluate the reliability of the sample.

Disadvantages

(a) This technique of sampling cannot be used for a large sample. It is applicable only for small sample.

(b) This technique is time consuming, costly, and requires more competition.

(c) Its planning and administration is more complicated.

Multi-Stage Sampling

This sample is more comprehensive and representative of the population. In this type of sampling primary sample units are inclusive groups and secondary units are sub-groups within these ultimate units to be selected which belong to one and only one group. Stages of a population are usually available within a group or population, whenever stratification is done by the researcher. The Individuals are selected from different stages for constituting the multi-stage sampling.

Advantages

(a) It is a good representative of the population.

(b) Multi-stage sampling is an improvement over the earlier methods.

(c) It is an objective procedure of sampling.

(d) The observations from multi-stage sample may be used for inferential purpose.

Disadvantages

(a) It is a difficult and complex method of samplings.

(b) It involves errors when we consider the primary and secondary stages.

(c) It is again a subjective phenomenon.

Cluster Sampling

To select the intact group as a whole is known as a Cluster sampling. In Cluster sampling the sample units contain groups of elements (clusters) instead of individual members or items in the population. Rather than listing all elementary school children in a given city and randomly selecting 15 per cent of these students for the sample, a researcher lists all of the elementary schools in the city, selects at random 15 per cent of these clusters of units, and uses all of the children in the selected schools as the sample.

Advantages

(a) It may be a good representative of the population.

(b) It is an easy method.

(c) It is an economical method.

(d) It is practicable and highly applicable in education.

(e) Observations can be used for inferential purpose.

Disadvantages

(a) Cluster sampling is not free from error.

(b) It is not comprehensive.

All these above are techniques of probability sampling.

Non-Probability Sampling Techniques

Non-probability is also known as non-parametric sampling which ate used for certain purpose.

1. Incidental or Accidental Assignment

The term incidental or accidental applied to those samples that are taken because they are most frequently available, i.e. this refers to groups which are used as samples of a population because they are readily available or because the researcher is unable to employ more acceptable sampling methods.

Advantages

(a) It is very easy method of sampling.
(b) It is frequently used in behavioural sciences.
(c) It reduces the time, money and energy i.e. it is an economical method.

Disadvantages

(a) It is not a representative of the population.
(b) It is not free from error.
(c) Parametric statistics cannot be used.

2. Judgement Sampling

This involves the selection of a group from the population on the basis of available information thought. It is to be representative of the total population. Or the selection of a group by intuition on the basis of criterion deemed to be self-evident. Generally investigator should take the judgement sample so this sampling is highly risky.

Advantages

(a) Knowledge of the investigator can be best used in this technique of sampling.
(b) This technique of sampling is also economical.

Disadvantages

(a) This technique is objective.
(b) It is not free from error.
(c) It includes uncontrolled variation.

(d) Inferential statistics cannot be used for the observations of this sampling, so generalization is not possible.

3. Purposive Sampling

The purposive sampling is selected by some arbitrary method because it is known to be representative of the total population, or it is known that it will produce well matched groups. The Idea is to pick out the sample in relation to some criterion, which are considered important for the particular study. This method is appropriate when the study places special emphasis upon the control of certain specific variables.

Advantages

    (a) Use of the best available knowledge concerning the sample subjects.

    (b) Better control of significant variables.

    (c) Sample groups data can be easily matched.

    (d) Homogeneity of subjects used in the sample.

Disadvantages

    (a) Reliability of the criterion is questionable.

    (b) Knowledge of population is essential.

    (c) Errors in classifying sampling subjects.

    (d) Inability to utilise the inferential parametric statistics.

    (e) Inability to make generalization concerning total population.

4. Quota Sampling

This combined both judgment sampling and probability sampling. The population is classified into several categories: on the basis of judgment or assumption or the previous knowledge, the proportion of population falling into each category is decided. Thereafter a quota of cases to be drawn is fixed and the observer is allowed to sample as he likes. Quota sampling is very arbitrary and likely to figure in Municipal surveys.

Advantages

    (a) It is an improvement over the judgment sampling.

(b) It is an easy sampling technique.

(c) It is most frequently used in social surveys.

Disadvantages

(a) It is not a representative sample.

(b) It is not free from error.

(c) It has the influence of regional geographical and social factors.

Since research design is a plan by which research samples may be selected from a population and under which experimental treatments are administered and controlled so that their effect upon the sample may be measured. Therefore, a second step in the establishment of an experimental design is to select the treatments that will be used to control sources of learning change in the sample subjects.

Sampling Error

Sampling Error is incurred when the statistical characteristics of a population are estimated from a subset, or sample, of that population. Since the sample does not include all members of the population, statistics on the sample, such as means and quantiles, generally differ from the characteristics of the entire population, which are known as parameters. For example, if one measures the height of a thousand individuals from a country of one million, the average height of the thousand is typically not the same as the average height of all one million people in the country. Since sampling is typically done to determine the characteristics of a whole population, the difference between the sample and population values is considered a *sampling error*.

Chapter 8

Data Collection

Data-Meaning

Data means observations or evidences. The scientific educational researches require the data by means of some standardized research tools or self-designed instrument. Data are both qualitative and quantitative in nature. Score is the numerical description of an individual with regard to some characteristics or variables. Measurement process is employed to quantify a variable. Data are collected for both variables as well as attributes. These are gathered in terms of frequency and scores. It depends on the type of instrument employed for its measurement. Generally tests yield the data in the form of scores and questionnaires provide the data in the form of frequency. Data are things with which we think of. Data and facts are used in educational research, therefore, it is essential to understand them clearly.

Nature of Data

The research studies in behavioral science or mainly concerned with the characteristics or traits. Thus, tools are administered to quantify these characteristics, but all traits or characteristics can not be Quantified.

The data can be classified into two broad categories:

1. Qualitative data or attributes.
2. Quantitative data or variables.

1. **Quantitative Data or Attributes:** The characteristics or traits for which numerical value can not be assigned, are called attributes, e.g. motivation, confidence, honesty integrity etc.

2. **Quantitative Data or Variables:** The characteristics or traits for which numerical value can be assigned, are called variables, e.g. Achievement Intelligena, Aptitude Height, Weight etc.

The distinction is based on the process of measurement rather than on the properties inherent in the phenomenon or trait, for generally properties considered qualitative can be made quantitative by measuring them with an instrument designed to assign numerical values to the various degrees to which they exist.

The decision to research a given phenomenon on the basis of its attributes or on the basis of its quantitative aspects is frequently a matter of choice, depending on such considerations as the need of precision and the ease of manipulation of data. In fact, the quantification of phenomenon is generally considered essential to the progress of a science particularly at the more advanced levels. Quantification provides a greater refinement and possesses definite advantages by virtue of its statistical treatment.

The quantitative data provide the nature of the characteristic or trait. They have the verbal exposition of the trait. There is much scope for logical manipulation is the interpretation of result. The trait is not quantifiable.

The qualitative data provide the extent and nature of the distribution of the trait or variable measured. The tools are available to measure the variable. In the experimental research data are collected in the controlled situation to study the functional relationship of variables.

Quantification is the process of assigning numerical values to the trait of the subjects of sample which normally would be quantitative. This can be done by:

(*a*) Observations or information by first hand experience. It is used in small children and animals.

(*b*) Systematic collection and analysis of factual data. This is done in historical research.

(*c*) Scales and inventories are designed to explore or reveal the interests, attitude and personality.

It is used in the case of study and survey research.

(d) Questionnaire, interview and opinionnaire are designed to gain information. This is employed in survey research.

(e) Educational and psychological tools are administered to quantify the variables more accurately. These tools are used in scientific research studies.

Various types of research tools are employed to collect the data. These tools yield different types of data.

Collection of Data

The task of data collection begins after a research problem has been defined and research design/plan chalked out. While deciding about the method of data collection to be used for the study, the researcher should keep in mind two types of data viz., primary and secondary. The *primary data* are those which are collected afresh and for the first time, and thus happen to be original in character. The *secondary data,* on the other hand, are those which have already been collected by someone else and which have already been passed through the statistical process. The researcher would have to decide which sort of data he would be using (thus collecting) for his study and accordingly he will have to select one or the other method of data collection. The methods of collecting primary and secondary data differ since primary data are to be originally collected, while in case of secondary data the nature of data collection work is merely that of compilation.

Collection of Primary Data

There are several methods of collecting primary data, particularly in surveys and descriptive researches. Important ones are: observation method, interview method, through questionnaires, through schedules, and other methods which include warranty cards; distributor audits; pantry audits; consumer panels; using mechanical devices; through projective techniques; depth interviews, and content analysis.

Observation Method

Under the observation method, the information is sought by way of investigator's own direct observation without asking from the respondent. For instance, in a study relating to consumer behaviour, the investigator instead of asking the brand of wrist watch used by the respondent, may himself look at the watch. The main advantage of this method is that subjective bias is eliminated, if observation is done accurately.

Secondly, the information obtained under this method relates to what is currently happening; it is not complicated by either the past behaviour or future intentions or attitudes. Thirdly, this method is independent of respondents' willingness to respond and as such is relatively less demanding of active cooperation on the part of respondents as happens to be the case in the interview or the questionnaire method. This method is particularly suitable in studies which deal with subjects (i.e., respondents) who are not capable of giving verbal reports of their feelings for one reason or the other However, observation method has various limitations.

Firstly, it is an expensive method. Secondly, the information provided by this method is very limited. Thirdly, sometimes unforeseen factors may interfere with the observational task. At times, the fact that some people are rarely accessible to direct observation creates obstacle for this method to collect data effectively.

Interview Method

The interview method of collecting data involves presentation of oral-verbal stimuli and reply in terms of oral-verbal responses. This method can be used through personal interviews and, if possible, through telephone interviews.

(a) *Personal interviews*: Personal interview method requires a person known as the interviewer asking questions generally in a face-to-face contact to the other person or persons. This sort of interview may be in the form of direct personal investigation or it may be indirect oral investigation. In the case of direct personal investigation the interviewer has to collect the information personally from the sources concerned. He has to be on the spot and has to meet people from whom data have to be collected.

This method is particularly suitable for intensive investigations. But in certain cases it may not be possible or worthwhile to contact directly the persons concerned or on account of the extensive scope of enquiry, the direct personal investigation technique may not be used. In such cases an indirect oral examination can be conducted under which the interviewer has to cross-examine other persons who are supposed to have knowledge about the problem under investigation and the information, obtained is recorded. Most of the commissions and committees appointed by government to carry on investigations make use of this method.

The method of collecting information through personal interviews is usually carried out in a structured way. As such we call the interviews as *structured interviews*. Such interviews involve the use of a set of predetermined questions and of highly standardised techniques of recording. Thus, the interviewer in a structured interview follows a rigid procedure laid down, asking questions in a form and order prescribed. As against it, the *unstructured interviews* are characterised by a flexibility of approach to questioning. Unstructured interviews do not follow a system of pre-determined questions and standardised techniques of recording information. In a non-structured interview, the nterviewer is allowed much greater freedom to ask, in case of need, supplementary questions or at times he may omit certain questions if the situation so requires. He may even change the sequence of questions. He has relatively greater freedom while recording the responses to include some aspects and exclude others. Unstructured interviews also demand deep knowledge and greater skill on the part of the interviewer. Unstructured interview, however, happens to be the central technique of collecting information in case of exploratory or formulative research studies. But in case of descriptive studies, we quite often use the technique of structured interview because of its being more economical, providing a safe basis for generalization and requiring relatively lesser skill on the part of the interviewer.

Focused interview is meant to focus attention on the given experience of the respondent and its effects. Under it the interviewer has the freedom to decide the manner and sequence in which the questions would be asked and has also the freedom to explore reasons and motives. The main task of the interviewer in case of a focused interview is to confine the respondent to a discussion of issues with which he seeks conversance. Such interviews are used generally in the development of hypotheses and constitute a major type of unstructured interviews.

The *clinical interview* is concerned with broad underlying feelings or motivations or with the course of individual's life experience. The method of eliciting information under it is generally left to the interviewer's discretion.

In case **of** *non-directive interview*, the interviewer's function is simply to encourage the respondent to talk about the given topic with a bare minimum of direct questioning. The interviewer often acts as a catalyst to a comprehensive expression of the respondents' feelings and beliefs and of the frame of reference within which such feelings and beliefs take on personal significance.

(b) *Telephone interviews:* This method of collecting information consists in contacting respondents on telephone itself. It is not a very widely used method, but plays important part in industrial surveys, particularly in developed regions.

Questionnaires

A questionnaire consists of a number of questions printed or typed in a definite order on a form or set of forms. The questionnaire is mailed to respondents who are expected to read and understand the questions and write down the reply in the space meant for the purpose in the questionnaire itself. The respondents have to answer the questions on their own. The method of collecting data by mailing the questionnaires to respondents is most extensively employed in various economic and business surveys. Before using this method, it is always advisable to conduct 'pilot study' (Pilot Survey) for testing the questionnaires Pilot survey is infact the replica and rehearsal of the main survey. Such a survey, being conducted by experts, brings to the light the weaknesses (if any) of the questionnaires and also of the survey techniques. From the experience gained in this way, improvement can be effected.

Main Aspects of a Questionnaire

1. *General Form:* So far as the general form of a questionnaire is concerned, it can either be structured or unstructured questionnaire. Structured questionnaires are those questionnaires in which there are definite, concrete and pre-determined questions. The questions are presented with exactly the same wording and in the same order

to all respondents. Resort is taken to this sort of standardization to ensure that all respondents reply to the same set of questions. The form of the question may be either closed (i.e., of the type 'yes' or 'no') or open (i.e., inviting free response) but should be stated in advance and not constructed during questioning. Structured questionnaires may also have fixed alternative questions in which responses of the informants are limited to the stated alternatives. Thus a highly structured questionnaire is one in which all questions and answers are specified and comments in the respondent's own words are held to the minimum. When these characteristics are not present in a questionnaire, it can be termed as unstructured or non-structured questionnaire. More specifically, we can say that in an unstructured questionnaire, the interviewer is provided with a general guide on the type of information to be obtained, but the exact question formulation is largely his own responsibility and the replies are to be taken down in the respondent's own words to the extent possible; in some situations tape recorders may be used to achieve this goal.

2. *Question Sequence:* In order to make the questionnaire effective and to ensure quality to the replies received, a researcher should pay attention to the question-sequence in preparing the questionnaire. A proper sequence of questions reduces considerably the chances of individual questions being misunderstood. The question-sequence must be clear and smoothly-moving, meaning thereby that the relation of one question to another should be readily apparent to the respondent, with questions that are easiest to answer being put in the beginning. The first few questions are particularly important because they are likely to influence the attitude of the respondent and in seeking his desired cooperation.

3. *Question Formulation and Wording:* With regard to this aspect of questionnaire, the researcher should note that each question must be very clear for any sort of misunderstanding can do irreparable harm to a survey. Question should also be impartial in order not to give a biased picture of the true state of affairs. Questions should be constructed with a view to their forming a logical part of a

well thought out tabulation plan. In general, all questions should meet the following standards—(a) should be easily understood; (b) should be simple i.e., should convey only one thought at a time; (c) should be concrete and should conform as much as possible to the respondent's way of thinking.

Essentials of a Good Questionnaire: To be successful, questionnaire should be comparatively short and simple i.e., the size of the questionnaire should be kept to the minimum. Questions should proceed in logical sequence moving from easy to more difficult questions. Personal and intimate questions should be left to the end. Technical terms and vague expressions capable of different interpretations should be avoided in a questionnaire. Questions may be dichotomous (yes or no answers), multiple choice (alternative answers listed) or open-ended. The latter type of questions are often difficult to analyse and hence should be avoided in a questionnaire to the extent possible.. There should always be provision for indications of uncertainty, e.g., "do not know," "no preference" and so on. Brief directions with regard to filling up the questionnaire should invariably be given in the questionnaire itself. Finally, the physical appearance of the questionnaire affects the cooperation the researcher receives from the recipients and as such an attractive looking questionnaire, particularly in mail surveys, is a plus point for enlisting cooperation. The quality of the paper, along with its colour, must be good so that it may attract the attention of recipients.

Collection of Data through Schedules

This method of data collection is very much like the collection of data through questionnaire, with little difference which lies in the fact that schedules (proforma containing a set of questions) are being filled in by the enumerators who are specially appointed for the purpose. These enumerators along with schedules, go to respondents, put to them the questions from the proforma in the order the questions are listed and record the replies in the space meant for the same in the proforma. In certain situations, schedules may be handed over to respondents and enumerators may help them in recording their answers to various questions in the said schedules.

This method of data collection is very useful in extensive enquiries and can lead to fairly reliable results. It is, however, very expensive and is usually adopted in investigations conducted by governmental agencies or by some big organisations. Population census all over the world is conducted through this method.

Difference between Questionnaire and Schedules

Both questionnaire and schedule are popularly used methods of collecting data in research surveys. There is much resemblance in the nature of these two methods and this fact has made many people to remark that from a practical point of view, the two methods can be taken to be the same. But from the technical point of view there is difference between the two. The important points of difference are as under:

1. The questionnaire is generally sent through mail to informants to be answered as specified in a covering letter, but otherwise without further assistance from the sender. The schedule is generally filled out by the research worker or the enumerator, who can interpret questions when necessary.

2. To collect data through questionnaire is relatively cheap and economical since we have to spend money only in preparing the questionnaire and in mailing the same to respondents. Here no field staff required. To collect data through schedules is relatively more expensive since considerable amount of money has to be spent in appointing enumerators and in importing training to them. Money is also spent in preparing schedules.

3. Non-response is usually high in case of questionnaire as many people do not respond and many return the questionnaire without answering all questions. Bias due to non-response often remains indeterminate. As against this, non-response is generally very low in case of schedules because these are filled by enumerators who are able to get answers to all questions. But there remains the danger of interviewer bias and cheating.

4. In case of questionnaire, it is not always clear as to who replies, but in case of schedule the identity of respondent is known.

5. The questionnaire method is likely to be very slow since many respondents do not return the questionnaire in time despite several

reminders, but in case of schedules the information is collected well in time as they are filled in by enumerators.

6. Personal contact is generally not possible in case of the questionnaire method as questionnaires are sent to respondents by post who also in turn return the same by post. But in case of schedules direct personal contact is established with respondents.
7. Questionnaire method can be used only when respondents are literate and cooperative, but in case of schedules the information can be gathered even when the respondents happen to be illiterate.
8. Wider and more representative distribution of sample is possible under the questionnaire method, but in respect of schedules there usually remains the difficulty in sending enumerators over a relatively wider area.
9. Risk of collecting incomplete and wrong information is relatively more under the questionnaire method, particularly when people are unable to understand questions properly. But in case of schedules, the information collected is generally complete and accurate as enumerators can remove the difficulties, if any, faced by respondents in correctly understanding the questions. As a result, the information collected through schedules is relatively more accurate than that obtained through questionnaires.
10. The success of questionnaire method lies more on the quality of the questionnaire itself, but in the case of schedules much depends upon the honesty and competence of enumerators.
11. In order to attract the attention of respondents, the physical appearance of questionnaire must be quite attractive, but this may not be so in case of schedules as they are to be filled in by enumerators and not by respondents.
12. Along with schedules, observation method can also be used but such a thing is not possible while collecting data through questionnaires.

Some Other Methods of Data Collection

1. **Warranty cards:** Warranty cards are usually postal sized cards which are used by dealers of consumer durables to collect information regarding their products. The information sought is printed in the

form of questions on the 'warranty cards' which is placed inside the package along with the product with a request to the consumer to fill in the card and post it back to the dealer.

2. **Distributor or store audits:** Distributor or store audits are performed by distributors as well as manufactures through their salesmen at regular intervals. Distributors get the retail stores audited through salesmen and use such information to estimate market size, market share, seasonal purchasing pattern and so on. The data are obtained in such audits not by questioning but by observation. For instance, in case of a grocery store audit, a sample of stores is visited periodically and data are recorded on inventories on hand either by observation or copying from store records. Store audits are invariably panel operations, for the derivation of sales estimates and compilation of sales trends by stores are their principal *'raison detre'*. The principal advantage of this method is that it offers the most efficient way of evaluating the effect on sales of variations of different techniques of in-store promotion.

3. **Pantry audits:** Pantry audit technique is used to estimate consumption of the basket of goods at the consumer level. In this type of audit, the investigator collects an inventory of types, quantities and prices of commodities consumed. Thus in pantry audit data are recorded from the examination of consumer's pantry. The usual objective in a pantry audit is to find out what types of consumers buy certain products and certain brands, the assumption being that the contents of the pantry accurately portray consumer's preferences. Quite often, pantry audits are supplemented by direct questioning relating to reasons and circumstances under which particular products were purchased in an attempt to relate these factors to purchasing habits. A pantry audit may or may not be set up as a panel operation, since a single visit is often considered sufficient to yield an accurate picture of consumers' preferences. An important limitation of pantry audit approach is that, at times, it may not be possible to identify consumers' preferences from the audit data alone, particularly when promotion devices produce a marked rise in sales.

4. **Consumer panels:** An extension of the pantry audit approach on a regular basis is known as 'consumer panel,' where a set of consumers are arranged to come to an understanding to maintain detailed daily records of their consumption and the same is made available to investigator on demands. In other words, a consumer panel is essentially a sample of consumers who are interviewed repeatedly over a period of time. Mostly consume panels are of two types viz., the transitory consumer panel and the continuing consumer panel.

   Transitory consumer panel is set up to measure the effect of a particular phenomenon. Usually such a panel is conducted on a before-and-after-basis. Initial interviews are conducted before the phenomenon takes place to record the attitude of the consumer. A second set of interviews is carried out after the phenomenon has taken place to find out the consequent changes that might have occurred in the consumer's attitude. It is a favourite tool of advertising and of social research.

   A *continuing consumer panel* is often set up for an indefinite period with a view to collect data on a particular aspect of consumer behaviour over time, generally at periodic intervals or may be meant to serve as a general purpose panel for researchers on a variety of subjects. Such panels have been used in the area of consumer expenditure, public opinion and radio and TV listenership among others. Most of these panels operate by mail. The representativeness of the panel relative to the population and the effect of panel membership on the information obtained after the two major problems associated with the use of this method of data collection.

5. **Use of mechanical devices:** The use of mechanical devices has been widely made to collect information by way of indirect means. Eye camera, Pupilometric camera, Psychogalvanometer, Motion picture camera and Audiometer are the principal devices so far developed and commonly used by modern big business houses, mostly in the developed world for the purpose of collecting the required information.

Eye cameras are designed to record the focus of eyes of a respondent on a specific portion of a sketch or diagram or written material. Such an information is useful in designing advertising material.

Pupilometric cameras record dilation of the pupil as a result of a visual stimulus. The extent of dilation shows the degree of interest aroused by the stimulus. Psychogalvanometer is used for measuring the extent of body excitement as a result of the visual stimulus. Motion picture cameras can be used to record movement of body of a buyer while deciding to buy a consumer good from a shop or big store. Influence of packaging or the information given on the label would stimulate a buyer to perform certain physical movements which can easily be recorded by a hidden motion picture camera in the shop's four walls. Audiometers are used by some TV concerns to find out the type of programmes as well as stations preferred by people. A device is fitted in the television instrument itself to record these changes. Such data may be used to find out the market share of competing television stations.

6. **Projective techniques:** Projective techniques (or what are sometimes called as indirect interviewing techniques) for the collection of data have been developed by psychologists to use projections of respondents for inferring about underlying motives, urges, or intentions which are such that the respondent either resists to reveal them or is unable to figure out himself. In projective techniques the respondent in supplying information tends unconsciously to project his own attitudes or feelings on the subject under study. Projective techniques play an important role in motivational researches or in attitude surveys.

The Important Projective Techniques

(i) *Word association tests:* These tests are used to extract information regarding such words which have maximum association. In this sort of test the respondent is asked to mention the first word that comes to mind, ostensibly without thinking, as the interviewer reads out each word from a list. If the interviewer says *cold*, the respondent may say *hot* and the like ones. The general technique is to use a list of as many as 50 to 100 words. Analysis of the matching words supplied by the respondents indicates whether the given word should be used for the contemplated purpose.

(ii) *Sentence completion tests:* These tests happen to be an extension of the technique of word association tests. Under this, informant may be asked to complete a sentence (such as: persons who wear Jeans are...) to find association of jeans clothes with certain personality characteristics. Several sentences of this type might be put to the informant on the same subject. Analysis of replies from the same informant reveals his attitude toward that subject, and the combination of these attitudes of all the sample members is then taken to reflect the views of the population.

(iii) *Story completion tests:* Such tests are a step further wherein the researcher may contrive stories instead of sentences and ask the informants to complete them. The respondent is given just enough of story to focus his attention on a given subject and he is asked to supply a conclusion to the story.

(iv) *Verbal projection tests:* These are the tests wherein the respondent is asked to comment on or to explain what other people do. For example, why do people smoke? Answers may reveal the respondent's own motivations.

(v) *Pictorial techniques:* There are several pictorial techniques. The important ones are as follows:

(a) *Thematic apperception test (T.A.T.):* The TAT consists of a set of pictures (some of the pictures deal with the ordinary day-to-day events while others may be ambiguous pictures of unusual situations) that are shown to respondents who are asked to describe what they think the pictures represent. The replies of respondents constitute the basis for the investigator to draw inferences about their personality structure, attitudes, etc.

(b) *Rosenzweig test:* This test uses a cartoon format wherein we have a series of cartoons with words inserted in 'balloons' above. The respondent is asked to put his own words in an empty balloon space provided for the purpose in the picture. From what the respondents write in this fashion, the study of their attitudes can be made.

(c) *Rorschach test:* This test consists of ten cards having prints of inkblots. The design happens to be symmetrical but meaningless. The respondents are asked to describe what they perceive in such symmetrical inkblots and the responses are interpreted on the basis of some pre-determined psychological framework. This test is frequently used but the problem of validity still remains a major problem of this test.

(d) *Holtzman Inkblot Test (HIT):* This test from W.H. Holtzman is a modification of the Rorschach Test explained above. This test consists of 45 inkblot cards which are based on colour, movement, shading and other factors involved in inkblot perception. Only one response per card is obtained from the subject (or the respondent) and the responses of a subject are interpreted at three levels of form appropriateness. Form responses are interpreted for knowing the accuracy (F) or inaccuracy (F–) of respondent's percepts; shading and colour for ascertaining his affectional and emotional needs; and movement responses for assessing the dynamic aspects of his life.

(e) *Tomkins-Horn picture arrangement test:* This test is designed for group administration. It consists of twenty-five plates, each containing three sketches that may be arranged in different ways to portray sequence of events. The respondent is asked to arrange them in a sequence which he considers as reasonable. The responses are interpreted as providing evidence confirming certain norms, respondent's attitudes, etc.

(vi) *Play techniques:* Under play techniques subjects are asked to improvise or act out a situation in which they have been assigned various roles. The researcher may observe such traits as hostility, dominance, sympathy, prejudice or the absence of such traits. These techniques have been used for knowing the attitudes of younger ones through manipulation of dolls. Dolls representing different racial groups are usually given to children who are allowed to play with them freely.

(vii) *Quizzes, tests and examinations:* This is also a technique of extracting information regarding specific ability of candidates indirectly. In this procedure both long and short questions are framed to test through them the memorising and analytical ability of candidates.

(viii) *Sociometry:* Sociometry is a technique for describing the social relationships among individuals in a group. In an indirect way, sociometry attempts to describe attractions or repulsions between individuals by asking them to indicate whom they would choose or reject in various situations.

7. **Depth interviews:** Depth interviews are those interviews that are designed to discover underlying motives and desires and are often used in motivational research. Such interviews are held to explore needs, desires and feelings of respondents. In other words, they aim to elicit unconscious as also other types of material relating especially to personality dynamics and motivations. As such, depth interviews require great skill on the part of the interviewer and at the same time involve considerable time. Unless the researcher has specialised training, depth interviewing should not be attempted.

8. **Content-analysis:** Content-analysis consists of analysing the contents of documentary materials such as books, magazines, newspapers and the contents of all other verbal materials which can be either spoken or printed.

Collection of Secondary Data

Secondary data means data that are already available i.e., they refer to the data which have already been collected and analysed by someone else. When the researcher utilises secondary data, then he has to look into various sources from where he can obtain them. In this case he is certainly not confronted with the problems that are usually associated with the collection of original data. Secondary data may either be published data or unpublished data. Usually published data are available in:

(a) Various publications of the central, state are local governments;
(b) Various publications of foreign governments or of international bodies and their subsidiary organisations;
(c) Technical and trade journals;
(d) Books, magazines and newspapers;
(e) Reports and publications of various associations connected with business and industry, banks, stock exchanges, etc.;
(f) Reports prepared by research scholars, universities, economists, etc. in different fields; and
(g) Public records and statistics, historical documents, and other sources of published information.

The sources of unpublished data are many; they may be found in diaries, letters, unpublished biographies and autobiographies and also may be available with scholars and research workers, trade associations, labour bureaus and other public/private individuals and organisations.

Researcher must be very careful in using secondary data. He must make a minute scrutiny because it is just possible that the secondary data may be unsuitable or may be inadequate in the context of the problem which the researcher wants to study. In this connection Dr. A.L. Bowley very aptly observes that it is never safe to take published statistics at their face value without knowing their meaning and limitations and it is always necessary to criticise arguments that can be based on them. By way of caution, the researcher, before using secondary data, must see that they possess following characteristics:

1. **Reliability of Data:** The reliability can be tested by finding out such things about the said data:
    (a) Who collected the data?

(b) What were the sources of data?
(c) Were they collected by using proper methods
(d) At what time were they collected?
(e) Was there any bias of the compiler?
(f) What level of accuracy was desired? Was it achieved?

2. **Suitability of Data:** The data that are suitable for one enquiry may not necessarily be found suitable in another enquiry. Hence, if the available data are found to be unsuitable, they should not be used by the researcher. In this context, the researcher must very carefully scrutinise the definition of various terms and units of collection used at the time of collecting the data from the primary source originally.

3. **Adequacy of Data:** If the level of accuracy achieved in data is found inadequate for the purpose of the present enquiry, they will be considered as inadequate and should not be used by the researcher. The data will also be considered inadequate, if they are related to an area which may be either narrower or wider than the area of the present enquiry.

Case Study Method

Meaning: The case study method is a very popular form of qualitative analysis and involves a careful and complete observation of a social unit, be that unit a person, a family, an institution, a cultural group or even the entire community. It is a method of study in depth rather than breadth. The case study places more emphasis on the full analysis of a limited number of events or conditions and their interrelations. The case study deals with the processes that take place and their interrelationship. Thus, case study is essentially an intensive investigation of the particular unit under consideration.

The object of the case study method is to locate the factors that account for the behaviour-patterns of the given unit as an integrated totality.

Characteristics: The important characteristics of the case study method are as under:

1. Under this method the researcher can take one single social unit or more of such units for his study purpose; he may even take a situation to study the same comprehensively.
2. Here the selected unit is studied intensively i.e., it is studied in minute details. Generally, the study extends over a long period of time to ascertain the natural history of the unit so as to obtain enough information for drawing correct inferences.
3. In the context of this method we make complete study of the social unit covering all facets. Through this method we try to understand the complex of factors that are operative within a social unit as an integrated totality.
4. Under this method the approach happens to be qualitative and not quantitative. Mere quantitative information is not collected. Every possible effort is made to collect information concerning all aspects
5. In respect of the case study method an effort is made to know the mutual inter-relationship of causal factors.
6. Under case study method the behaviour pattern of the concerning unit is studied directly and not by an indirect and abstract approach.
7. Case study method results in fruitful hypotheses along with the data which may be helpful in testing them, and thus it enables the generalised knowledge to get richer and richer. In its absence, generalised social science may get handicapped.

Major Phases Involved: Major phases involved in case study are as follows:

(i) Recognition and determination of the status of the phenomenon to be investigated or the unit of attention.

(ii) Collection of data, examination and history of the given phenomenon.

(iii) Diagnosis and identification of causal factors as a basis for remedial or developmental treatment.

(iv) Application of remedial measures i.e., treatment and therapy (this phase is often characterized as case work).

(v) Follow-up programme to determine effectiveness of the treatment applied.

Chapter 9

Data Analysis

The analysis and interpretation of data represent the application of deductive and inductive logic to the research process. The data are often classified by division into, subgroups, and are then analyzed and synthesized in such a way that hypothesis may be verified or rejected. The final result may be a new principle or generalization. Data are examined in terms of comparison between the more homogeneous segments within the group any by comparison with some outside criteria.

Analysis of data includes comparison of the outcomes of the various treatments upon the several groups and the making of a decision as to the achievement of the goals of research. Data relevant to each hypothesis must be assembled in quantitative form and tested to determine whether or not there is a significant difference in the results obtained from the controlled groups. Usually the analysis develops as a comparison between groups however, sometimes the type of data obtainable tends itself better to the existing differences by contrast or by summing up.

The collected data are known as 'raw data'. The raw data are meaningless unless certain statistical treatment is given to them. Analysis of data means to make the raw data meaningful or to draw some results from the data after the proper treatment. The 'null hypotheses' are tested with the help of analysis data so to obtain some significant results.

Analysis of Data

Analysis of data means studying the tabulated material in order to determine inherent facts or meanings. It involves breaking down existing complex factors into simpler parts and putting the parts together in new arrangements for the purpose of interpretation. A plan of analysis can and should be prepared in advance before the actual collection of material. A preliminary analysis on the skeleton plan should as the investigation proceeds, develop into a complete final analysis enlarged and reworked as and when necessary. This process requires an alert, flexible and open mind. Caution is necessary at every step. In case where a plan of analysis has not been made beforehand. There are four helpful modes to get started on analyzing the gathered data:

1. To think in terms of significant tables that the data permit.
2. To examine carefully the statement of the problem and the earlier analysis and to study the original records of the data.
3. To get away from the data and to think about the problem in layman's terms.
4. To attack the data by making various simple statistical calculations.

In the general process of analysis of research data, statistical method has contributed a great deal.

Simple statistical calculation finds a place in almost any research study dealing with large or even small groups of individuals, while complex statistical computations form the basis of many types of research.

Types of Analysis of Data

Statistics is the body of mathematical techniques or processes for gathering, describing organizing and interpreting numerical data. Since research often yields such quantitative data, statistics is a basic tool of measurement and research. The research worker who uses statistics is concerned with more than the manipulation of data, statistical methods goes back to fundamental purposes of analysis. Research may deal with different types of statistical data application.

1. Descriptive Statistical Analysis
2. Correlation Analysis
3. Causal Analysis
4. Multivariate Analysis
5. Inferential Statistical Analysis.

Descriptive Statistical Analysis

Descriptive statistical analysis is concerned with numerical description of a particular group observed and any similarity to those outside the group cannot be taken for granted. The data describe one group and that one group only. Much simple educational research involves descriptive statistics and provides valuable information about the nature of a particular group or class.

Descriptive study provides us with profiles of companies, work groups, persons and other subjects on any of a multiple of characteristics such as size. Composition, efficiency, preferences, etc. this sort of analysis may be in respect of one variable (described as unidimensional analysis), or in respect of two variables (described as bivariate analysis) or in respect of more than two variables (described as multivariate analysis).

Correlation Analysis

Correlation analysis studies the joint variation of two or more variables for determining the amount of correlation between two or more variables.

Causal Analysis

Causal analysis is concerned with the study of how one or more variables affect changes in another variable. It is thus a study of functional relationships existing between two or more variables. This analysis can be termed as regression analysis. Causal analysis is considered relatively more important in experimental researches, whereas in most social and business researches our interest lies in understanding and controlling relationships between variables then with determining causes *per se* and as such we consider correlation analysis as relatively more important.

Multivariate Analysis

In modern times, with the availability of computer facilities, there has been a rapid development of *multivariate analysis* which may be defined as "all statistical methods which simultaneously analyse more than two variables on a sample of observations". Usually the following analyses are involved when we make a reference of multivariate analysis:

(a) *Multiple Regression Analysis:* This analysis is adopted when the researcher has one dependent variable which is presumed to be a function of two or more independent variables. The objective of this analysis is to make a prediction about the dependent variable based on its covariance with all the concerned independent variables.

(b) *Multiple Discriminant Analysis:* This analysis is appropriate when the researcher has a single dependent variable that cannot be measured, but can be classified into two or more groups on the basis of some attribute. The object of this analysis happens to be to predict an entity's possibility of belonging to a particular group based on several predictor variables.

(c) *Multivariate Analysis of Variance (or multi-ANOVA)*: This analysis is an extension of twoway ANOVA, wherein the ratio of among group variance to within group variance is worked out on a set of variables.

(d) *Canonical Analysis:* This analysis can be used in case of both measurable and non-measurable variables for the purpose of simultaneously predicting a set of dependent variables from their joint covariance with a set of independent variables.

Inferential Statistical Analysis

Inferential statistical analysis involves the process of sampling, the selection for study of a small group that is assumed to be related to the large group from which it is drawn. The small group is known as the sample; the large group, the population or universe, A statistic is a measure based on a sample. A statistic computed from a sample may be used to estimate a parameter, the corresponding value in the population which it is selected.

Analysis of data can be summarized in a broad general way as follows

Analysis of Data

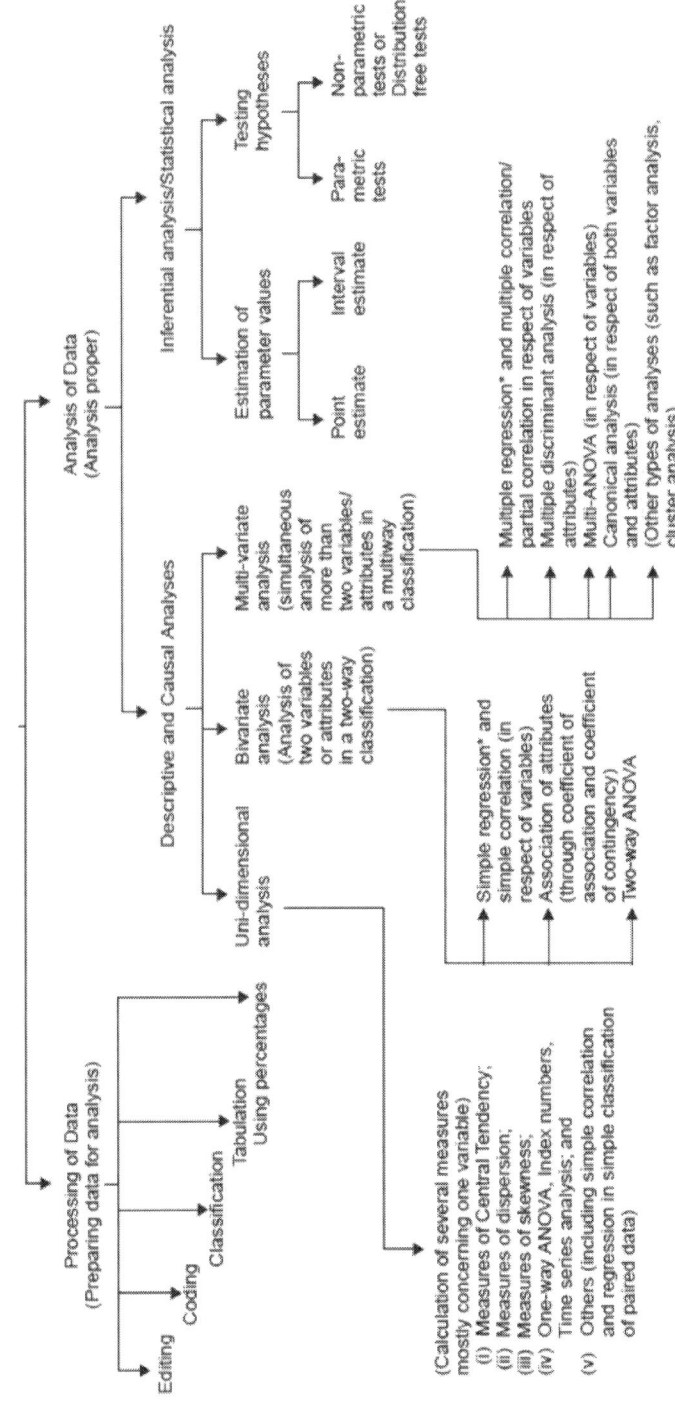

Source: Kothari.C.R (2004), Research Methodology: Methods & Techniques

Descriptive Data Analysis

Data collected from tests and experiments often have little meaning or significance until they have been classified or rearranged in a systematic way. Descriptive statistics concern the development of certain indices from the raw data, whereas inferential statistics concern with the process of generalisation.

The important statistical measures that are used to summarise the survey/research data are:

(1) Measures of central tendency or statistical averages;

(2) Measures of dispersion;

(3) Measures of asymmetry (skewness);

(4) Measures of relationship; and

(5) Other measures.

Amongst the measures of central tendency, the three most important ones are the arithmetic average or mean, median and mode. Geometric mean and harmonic mean are also sometimes used.

From among the measures of dispersion, variance, and its square root—the standard deviation are the most often used measures. Other measures such as mean deviation, range, etc. are also used. For comparison purpose, we use mostly the coefficient of standard deviation or the coefficient of variation.

In respect of the measures of skewness and kurtosis, we mostly use the first measure of skewness based on mean and mode or on mean and median. Other measures of skewness, based on quartiles or on the methods of moments, are also used sometimes. Kurtosis is also used to measure the peakedness of the curve of the frequency distribution.

Amongst the measures of relationship, Karl Pearson's coefficient of correlation is the frequently used measure in case of statistics of variables, whereas Yule's coefficient of association is used in case of statistics of attributes. Multiple correlation coefficient, partial correlation coefficient, regression analysis, etc., are other important measures often used by a researcher.

Index numbers, analysis of time series, coefficient of contingency, etc., are other measures that may as well be used by a researcher, depending upon the nature of the problem under study.

Inferential Data Analysis

The primary purpose of research is to discover principles' that have universal application. But to study a whole population in order to arrive at generalization would be impracticable if not impossible. A measured value based upon sample data is statistic. A population value estimated from a statistic is a parameter. A sample is a small proportion of a population selected for analysis. By observing the sample, certain inferences may be made about the population. Samples are not selected haphazardly, but are chosen in a deliberate way so that the influence of chance or probability can be estimated. Several types of sampling procedures are there and each one is particularly appropriate in a given set of circumstances. Inferential statistics are also known as sampling statistics and are mainly concerned with two major type of problems: (i) the estimation of population parameters, and (ii) the testing of statistical hypotheses.

Inference from Statistics to Parameters

The basic ideas of inference are to estimate the parameters with the help of sample statistics which play an extremely important role in educational research. These basic ideals of which the concept of underlying distribution is a part, comprise the foundation for testing hypotheses using statistical techniques.

The chain of reasoning from statistics to parameters is a part of what we call inferential statistics. The inference is from the statistics to the parameters We have a population and we want to know something about the descriptive measures of this population, namely the parameters. It is desirable or impossible to measure the entire population, so a random sample is selected from the population. The descriptive measures of the sample are known as statistics and the statistics can be determined. Since the sample is a random sample, we know that the statistics can be employed to estimate the population parameters within fluctuation due to sampling. It is at this point that the underlying distribution of the statistics comes in. If we know the underlying distributions we know how the statistics behaves. The appropriate underlying distribution for a specific statistics has been determined for us by mathematical theory and has been tabulated in table form.

Underlying distributions are commonly theoretical distributions. The parameters are never known for certain unless the entire population is measured and then there is no inference. We look at the statistics and their underlying distributions and from them we reason to tenable conclusions about the parameters.

Descriptive Data Analysis Explained

Measures of Central Tendency

Measures of central tendency (or statistical averages) tell us the point about which items have a tendency to cluster. Such a measure is considered as the most representative figure for the entire mass of data. Measure of central tendency is also known as statistical average. Mean, median and mode are the most popular averages. *Mean,* also known as arithmetic average, is the most common measure of central tendency and may be defined as the value which we get by dividing the total of the values of various given items in a series by the total number of items. we can work it out as under:

$$\text{Mean (or } \bar{X})^* = \frac{\Sigma X_i}{n} = \frac{X_1 + X_2 + ... + X_n}{n}$$

where $\bar{X}$ = The symbol we use for mean (pronounced as X bar)
Σ = Symbol for summation
X_i = Value of the ith item X, $i = 1, 2, ..., n$
n = total number of items

In case of a frequency distribution, we can work out mean in this way:

$$\bar{X} = \frac{\Sigma f_i X_i}{\Sigma f_i} = \frac{f_1 X_1 + f_2 X_2 + ... + f_n X_n}{f_1 + f_2 + ... + f_n = n}$$

Sometimes, instead of calculating the simple mean, as stated above, we may workout the weighted mean for a realistic average. The weighted mean can be worked out as follows:

$$\bar{X}_w = \frac{\Sigma w_i X_i}{\Sigma w_i}$$

where $\bar{X}_w$ = Weighted item
w_i = weight of ith item X
X_i = value of the ith item X

Mean is the simplest measurement of central tendency and is a widely used measure. Its chief use consists in summarising the essential features of a series and in enabling data to be compared. It is amenable to algebraic treatment and is used in further statistical calculations. It is a relatively stable measure of central tendency. But it suffers from some limitations viz., it is unduly affected by extreme items; it may not coincide with the actual value of an item in a series, and it may lead to wrong impressions, particularly when the item values are not given with the average.

Median is the value of the middle item of series when it is arranged in ascending or descending order of magnitude. It divides the series into two halves; in one half all items are less than median, whereas in the other half all items have values higher than median. If the values of the items arranged in the ascending order are: 60, 74, 80, 90, 95, 100, then the value of the 4th item viz., 88 is the value of median.

Median is a positional average and is used only in the context of qualitative phenomena, for example, in estimating intelligence, etc., which are often encountered in sociological fields. Median is not useful where items need to be assigned relative importance and weights. It is not frequently used in sampling statistics.

Mode is the most commonly or frequently occurring value in a series. The mode in a distribution is that item around which there is maximum concentration. In general, mode is the size of the item which has the maximum frequency, but at items such an item may not be mode on account of the effect of the frequencies of the neighbouring items. Like median, mode is a positional average and is not affected by the values of extreme items. it is, therefore, useful in all situations where we want to eliminate the effect of extreme variations. Mode is particularly useful in the study of popular sizes. For example, a manufacturer of readymade garments is usually interested in finding out the size most in demand so that he may manufacture a larger quantity of that size. In other words, he wants a modal size to be determined for median or mean size would not serve his purpose. but there are certain limitations of mode as well. For example, it is not amenable to algebraic treatment and sometimes remains indeterminate when we have two or more model values in a series. It is considered unsuitable in cases where we want to give relative importance to items under consideration.

Geometric mean is also useful under certain conditions. It is defined as the nth root of the product of the values of n times in a given series.

Harmonic mean is defined as the reciprocal of the average of reciprocals of the values of items of a series.

From what has been stated above, we can say that there are several types of statistical averages. Researcher has to make a choice for some average. There are no hard and fast rules for the selection of a particular average in statistical analysis for the selection of an average mostly depends on the nature, type of objectives of the research study. One particular type of average cannot be taken as appropriate for all types of studies. The chief characteristics and the limitations of the various averages must be kept in view; discriminate use of average is very essential for sound statistical analysis.

Measures of Dispersion

An averages can represent a series only as best as a single figure can, but it certainly cannot reveal the entire story of any phenomenon under study. Specially it fails to give any idea about the scatter of the values of items of a variable in the series around the true value of average. In order to measure this scatter, statistical devices called measures of dispersion are calculated. Important measures of dispersion are (a) range, (b) mean deviation, and (c) standard deviation.

(a) *Range* is the simplest possible measure of dispersion and is defined as the difference between the values of the extreme items of a series. Thus,

$$\text{Range} = \begin{pmatrix} \text{Highest value of an} \\ \text{item in a series} \end{pmatrix} - \begin{pmatrix} \text{Lowest value of an} \\ \text{item in a series} \end{pmatrix}$$

The utility of range is that it gives an idea of the variability very quickly, but the drawback is that range is affected very greatly by fluctuations of sampling. Its value is never stable, being based on only two values of the variable. As such, range is mostly used as a rough measure of variability and is not considered as an appropriate measure in serious research studies.

(b) *Mean deviation* is the average of difference of the values of items from some average of the series. Such a difference is technically described as deviation. In calculating mean deviation we ignore the minus sign of deviations while taking their total for obtaining the mean deviation.

(c) *Standard deviation* is most widely used measure of dispersion of a series and is commonly denoted by the symbol 'σ' (pronounced as sigma). Standard deviation is defined as the square-root of the average of squares of deviations, when such deviations for the values of individual items in a series are obtained from the arithmetic average. It is worked out as under:

$$\text{Standard deviation}^* (\sigma) = \sqrt{\frac{\Sigma(X_i - \bar{X})^2}{n}}$$

Or

$$\text{Standard deviation}(\sigma) = \sqrt{\frac{\Sigma f_i(X_i - \bar{X})^2}{\Sigma f_i}}, \text{ in case of frequency distribution}$$

When we divide the standard deviation by the arithmetic average of the series, the resulting quantity is known as *coefficient of standard deviation* which happens to be a relative measure and is often used for comparing with similar measure of other series. When this coefficient of standard deviation is multiplied by 100, the resulting figure is known as *coefficient of variation*. Sometimes, we work out the square of standard deviation, known as *variance*, which is frequently used in the context of analysis of variation.

The standard deviation (along with several related measures like variance, coefficient of variation, etc.) is used mostly in research studies and is regarded as a very satisfactory measure of dispersion in a series. It is amenable to mathematical manipulation because the algebraic signs are not ignored in its calculation (as we ignore in case of mean deviation). It is less affected by fluctuations of sampling. These advantages make standard deviation and its coefficient a very popular measure of the scatteredness of a series. It is popularly used in the context of estimation and testing of hypotheses.

Measure of Asymmetry (Skewness)

When the distribution of item in a series happens to be perfectly symmetrical, we then have the following type of curve for the distribution:

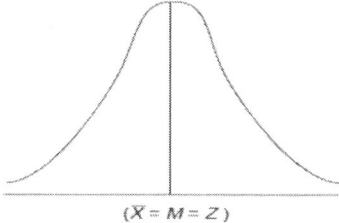

$(\bar{X} = M = Z)$

Such a curve is technically described as a *normal curve* and the relating distribution as normal distribution. Such a curve is perfectly bell shaped curve in which case the value of X or M or Z is just the same and skewness is altogether absent. But if the curve is distorted (whether on the right side or on the left side), we have asymmetrical distribution which indicates that there is skewness. If the curve is distorted on the right side, we have positive skewness but when the curve is distorted towards left, we have negative skewness as shown here under:

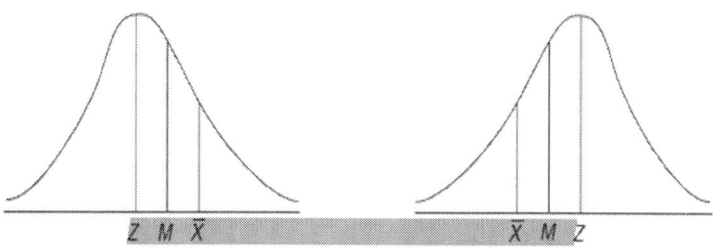

Curve showing positive skewness
In case of positive skewness we have:
$Z < M < \bar{X}$

Curve showing negative skewness
In case of negative skewness we have:
$\bar{X} < M < Z$

Skewness is, thus, a measure of asymmetry and shows the manner in which the items are clustered around the average. In a symmetrical distribution, the items show a perfect balance on either side of the mode, but in a skew distribution the balance is thrown to one side. The amount by which the balance exceeds on one side measures the skewness of the series. The difference between the mean, median or the mode provides an easy way of expressing skewness in a series. In case of positive skewness, we have $Z < M < X$ and in case of negative skewness we have $X < M < Z$.

Usually we measure skewness in this way:

$$\text{Skewness} = \overline{X} - Z \text{ and its coefficient } (j) \text{ is worked out as } j = \frac{\overline{X} - Z}{\sigma}$$

In case Z is not well defined, then we work out skewness as under:

$$\text{Skewness} = 3(\overline{X} - M) \text{ and its coefficient } (j) \text{ is worked out as } j = \frac{3(\overline{X} - M)}{\sigma}$$

The significance of skewness lies in the fact that through it one can study the formation of series and can have the idea about the shape of the curve, whether normal or otherwise, when the items of a given series are plotted on a graph.

Kurtosis is the measure of flat-toppedness of a curve. A bell shaped curve or the normal curve is Mesokurtic because it is kurtic in the centre; but if the curve is relatively more peaked than the normal curve, it is called Leptokurtic whereas a curve is more flat than the normal curve, it is called Platykurtic. In brief, Kurtosis is the humpedness of the curve and points to the nature of distribution of items in the middle of a series. It may be pointed out here that knowing the shape of the distribution curve is crucial to the use of statistical methods in research analysis since most methods make specific assumptions about the nature of the distribution curve.

Measures of Relationship

So far we have dealt with those statistical measures that we use in context of univariate population i.e., the population consisting of measurement of only one variable. But if we have the data on two variables, we are said to have a bivariate population and if the data happen to be on more than two variables, the population is known as multivariate population. If for every measurement of a variable, X, we have corresponding value of a second variable, Y, the resulting pairs of values are called a bivariate population. In addition, we may also have a corresponding value of the third variable, Z, or the forth variable, *W*, and so on, the resulting pairs of values are called a multivariate population. In case of bivariate or multivariate populations, we often wish to know the relation of the two and/or more variables in the data to one another. There are several methods of determining the relationship between variables, but no method can tell us for certain that a correlation is indicative of causal relationship. Thus we have to answer two types of questions in bivariate or multivariate populations viz.,

(i) Does there exist association or correlation between the two (or more) variables? If yes, of what degree?

(ii) Is there any cause and effect relationship between the two variables in case of the bivariate population or between one variable on one side and two or more variables on the other side in case of multivariate population? If yes, of what degree and in which direction?

The first question is answered by the use of correlation technique and the second question by the technique of regression. There are several methods of applying the two techniques, but the important ones are as under:

In case of bivariate population: Correlation can be studied through

(a) Cross tabulation;

(b) Charles Spearman's coefficient of correlation;

(c) Karl Pearson's coefficient of correlation;

whereas cause and effect relationship can be studied through simple regression equations.

In case of multivariate population: Correlation can be studied through

(a) Coefficient of multiple correlation;

(b) Coefficient of partial correlation;

whereas cause and effect relationship can be studied through multiple regression equations.

Cross tabulation approach is specially useful when the data are in nominal form. Under it we classify each variable into two or more categories and then cross classify the variables in these subcategories. Then we look for interactions between them which may be symmetrical, reciprocal or asymmetrical. A symmetrical relationship is one in which the two variables vary together, but we assume that neither variable is due to the other. A reciprocal relationship exists when the two variables mutually influence or reinforce each other. Asymmetrical relationship is said to exist if one variable (the independent variable) is responsible for another variable (the dependent variable). The cross classification procedure begins with a two-way table which indicates whether there is or there is not an interrelationship between the variables. This sort of analysis can be further elaborated in which case a third factor is introduced into the association through cross-classifying the three variables. By doing so we find conditional relationship in which factor X appears to affect factor Y only when factor Z is held constant.

Charles Spearman's coefficient of correlation (or rank correlation) is the technique of determining the degree of correlation between two variables in case of ordinal data where ranks are given to the different values of the variables. The main objective of this coefficient is to determine the extent to which the two sets of ranking are similar or dissimilar. This coefficient is determined as under:

$$\text{Spearman's coefficient of correlation (or } r_s) = 1 - \left[\frac{6\Sigma d_i^2}{n(n^2-1)}\right]$$

where d_i = difference between ranks of *i*th pair of the two variables;
       n = number of pairs of observations.

Karl Pearson's coefficient of correlation (or simple correlation) is the most widely used method of measuring the degree of relationship between two variables. This coefficient assumes the following:

(i) That there is linear relationship between the two variables;

(ii) That the two variables are casually related which means that one of the variables is independent and the other one is dependent; and

(iii) A large number of independent causes are operating in both variables so as to produce a normal distribution.

Karl Pearson's coefficient of correlation can be worked out thus.

Data Analysis 123

$$\text{Karl Pearson's coefficient of correlation (or } r\text{)}^* = \frac{\Sigma(X_i - \bar{X})(Y_i - \bar{Y})}{n \cdot \sigma_X \cdot \sigma_Y}$$

where X_i = ith value of X variable

X = mean of X

Y_i = ith value of Y variable

Y = Mean of Y

n = number of pairs of observations of X and Y

σX = Standard deviation of X

σY = Standard deviation of Y

Karl Pearson's coefficient of correlation is also known as the product moment correlation coefficient. The value of 'r' lies between ± 1. Positive values of r indicate positive correlation between the two variables (i.e., changes in both variables take place in the statement direction), whereas negative values of 'r' indicate negative correlation i.e., changes in the two variables taking place in the opposite directions. A zero value of 'r' indicates that there is no association between the two variables. When $r = (+) 1$, it indicates perfect positive correlation and when it is $(-)1$, it indicates perfect negative correlation, meaning thereby that variations in independent variable (X) explain 100% of the variations in the dependent variable (Y). We can also say that for a unit change in independent variable, if there happens to be a constant change in the dependent variable in the same direction, then correlation will be termed as perfect positive. But if such change occurs in the opposite direction, the correlation will be termed as perfect negative. The value of 'r' nearer to +1 or –1 indicates high degree of correlation between the two variables.

Simple Regression Analysis

Regression is the determination of a statistical relationship between two or more variables. In simple regression, we have only two variables, one variable (defined as independent) is the cause of the behaviour of another one (defined as dependent variable). Regression can only interpret what exists physically i.e., there must be a physical way in which independent variable X can affect dependent variable Y. The basic relationship between X and Y is given by

$$Y = a + bX$$

where the symbol Y denotes the estimated value of Y for a given value of X. This equation is known as the regression equation of Y on X (also represents the regression line of Y on X when drawn on a graph) which means that each unit change in X produces a change of b in Y, which is positive for direct and negative for inverse relationships.

Multiple Correlation and Regression

When there are two or more than two independent variables, the analysis concerning relationship is known as multiple correlation and the equation describing such relationship as the multiple regression equation. We here explain multiple correlation and regression taking only two independent variables and one dependent variable (Convenient computer programs exist for dealing with a great number of variables). In this situation the results are interpreted as shown below:

Multiple regression equation assumes the form

$$Y = a + b1X1 + b2X2$$

where X1 and X2 are two independent variables and Y being the dependent variable, and the constants a, b1 and b2 can be solved by solving the following three normal equations:

$$\sum Y_i = na + b_1 \sum X_{1i} + b_2 \sum X_{2i}$$
$$\sum X_{1i} Y_i = a \sum X_{1i} + b_1 \sum X_{1i}^2 + b_2 \sum X_{1i} X_{2i}$$
$$\sum X_{2i} Y_i = a \sum X_{2i} + b_1 \sum X_{1i} X_{2i} + b_2 \sum X_{2i}^2$$

(It may be noted that the number of normal equations would depend upon the number of independent variables. If there are 2 independent variables, then 3 equations, if there are 3 independent variables then 4 equations and so on, are used.)

In multiple regression analysis, the regression coefficients (viz., b1 b2) become less reliable as the degree of correlation between the independent variables (viz., X1, X2) increases. If there is a high degree of correlation between independent variables, we have a problem of what is commonly described as the *problem of multicollinearity*. In such a situation we should use only one set of the independent variable to make our estimate. In fact, adding a second variable, say $X2$, that is correlated with the first variable, say $X1$, distorts the values of the regression coefficients. Nevertheless, the prediction for the dependent variable can be made even when multicollinearity is present, but in such a situation enough care should be taken in selecting the independent variables to estimate a dependent variable so as to ensure that multi-collinearity is reduced to the minimum.

Partial Correlation

Partial correlation measures separately the relationship between two variables in such a way that the effects of other related variables are eliminated. In other words, in partial correlation analysis, we aim at measuring the relation between a dependent variable and a particular independent variable by holding all other variables constant. Thus, each partial coefficient of correlation measures the effect of its independent variable on the dependent variable. To obtain it, it is first necessary to compute the simple coefficients of correlation between each set of pairs of variables as stated earlier.

Other Measures

1. **Index Numbers:** When series are expressed in same units, we can use averages for the purpose of comparison, but when the units in which two or more series are expressed happen to be different, statistical averages cannot be used to compare them. In such situations we have to rely upon some relative measurement which consists in reducing the figures to a common base. Once such method is to convert the series into a series of index numbers. This is done when we express the given figures as percentages of some specific figure on a certain data. We can, thus, define an index number as a number which is used to measure the level of a given phenomenon as compared to the level of the same phenomenon at some standard date. The use of index number weights more as a special type of average, meant to study the changes in the effect of such factors which are incapable of being measured directly.

But one must always remember that index numbers measure only the relative changes.

Changes in various economic and social phenomena can be measured and compared through index numbers. Different indices serve different purposes. Specific commodity indices are to serve as a measure of changes in the phenomenon of that commodity only. Index numbers may measure cost of living of different classes of people. In economic sphere, index numbers are often termed as 'economic barometers measuring the economic phenomenon in all its aspects either directly by measuring the same phenomenon or indirectly by measuring something else which reflects upon the main phenomenon.

2. **Time Series Analysis:** In the context of economic and business researches, we may obtain quite often data relating to some time period concerning a given phenomenon. Such data is labelled as 'Time Series.' More clearly it can be stated that series of successive observations of the given phenomenon over a period of time are referred to as time series. Such series are usually the result of the effects of one or more of the following factors:

   (i) *Secular trend* or long term trend that shows the direction of the series in a long period of time. The effect of trend (whether it happens to be a growth factor or a decline factor) is gradual, but extends more or less consistently throughout the entire period of time under consideration. Sometimes, secular trend is simply stated as trend (or T).

   (ii) *Short time oscillations* i.e., changes taking place in the short period of time only and such changes can be the effect of the following factors:

   (a) *Cyclical fluctuations* (*or C*) are the fluctuations as a result of business cycles and are generally referred to as long term movements that represent consistently recurring rises and declines in an activity.

   (b) *Seasonal fluctuations* (*or S*) are of short duration occurring in a regular sequence at specific intervals of time. Such fluctuations are the result of changing seasons. Usually these fluctuations involve patterns of change within a year that tend to be repeated from year to year. Cyclical fluctuations and seasonal fluctuations taken together constitute short-period regular fluctuations.

(c) *Irregular fluctuations* (or *I*), also known as Random fluctuations, are variations which take place in a completely unpredictable fashion. All these factors stated above are termed as components of time series and when we try to analyse time series, we try to isolate and measure the effects of various types of these factors on a series. To study the effect of one type of factor, the other type of factor is eliminated from the series. The given series is, thus, left with the effects of one type of factor only.

For analysing time series, we usually have two models; (1) multiplicative model; and (2) additive model. Multiplicative model assumes that the various components interact in a multiplicative manner to produce the given values of the overall time series and can be stated as under:

$$Y = T \times C \times S \times I$$

where,

Y = observed values of time series,

T = Trend,

C = Cyclical fluctuations,

S = Seasonal fluctuations,

I = Irregular fluctuations.

Additive model considers the total of various components resulting in the given values of the overall time series and can be stated as:

$$Y = T + C + S + I$$

There are various methods of isolating trend from the given series viz., the free hand method, semiaverage method, method of moving averages, method of least squares and similarly there are methods of measuring cyclical and seasonal variations and whatever variations are left over are considered as random or irregular fluctuations.

The analysis of time series is done to understand the dynamic conditions for achieving the short term and long-term goals of business firm(s). The past trends can be used to evaluate the success or failure of management policy or policies practiced hitherto. On the basis of past trends, the future patterns can be predicted and policy or policies may accordingly be formulated. We can as well study properly the effects of factors causing changes in the short period of time only, once we have eliminated the effects of trend. By studying cyclical variations, we can keep in view the impact ofcyclical changes while formulating various policies to make them as realistic as possible. The knowledge of seasonal variations will be of great help to us in taking decisions regarding inventory, production, purchases and sales policies so as to optimize working results. Thus, analysis of time series is important in context of long term as well as short term forecasting and is considered a very powerful tool in the hands of business analysts and researchers.

Additional Note

Types of Data & Measurement Scales: Nominal, Ordinal, Interval and Ratio

There are four measurement scales (or types of data): nominal, ordinal, interval and ratio. These are simply ways to categorize different types of variables. These four measurement scales (nominal, ordinal, interval, and ratio) are best understood with example, as you'll see below.

Nominal

Nominal scales are used for labeling variables, without any quantitative value. "Nominal" scales could simply be called "labels." Here are some examples, below. Notice that all of these scales are mutually exclusive (no overlap) and none of them have any numerical significance. A good way to remember all of this is that "nominal" sounds a lot like "name" and nominal scales are kind of like "names" or labels.

Gender – Male/Female

Color – Red/Green/yellow

Residence – Adama/AddisAbaba/Jimma

Ordinal

With ordinal scales, it is the order of the values is what's important and significant, but the differences between each one is not really known. Ordinal scales are typically measures of non-numeric concepts like satisfaction, happiness, discomfort, etc.

"Ordinal" is easy to remember because is sounds like "order" and that's the key to remember with "ordinal scales"–it is the *order* that matters, but that's all you really get from these.

Feeling – Very unhappy/unhappy/neutral/happy/very happy

Satisfaction – very satisfied/satisfied/neither satisfied nor dissatisfied/dissatisfied/very much dissatisfied

Interval

Interval scales are numeric scales in which we know not only the order, but also the exact differences between the values. The classic example of an interval scale is Celsius temperature because the difference between each value is the same. For example, the difference between 60 and 50 degrees is a measurable 10 degrees, as is the difference between 80 and 70 degrees. Time is another good example of an interval scale in which the increments are known, consistent, and measurable. "Interval" itself means "space in between," which is the important thing to remember–interval scales not only tell us about order, but also about the value between each item.

Provides:	Nominal	Ordinal	Interval	Ratio
The "order" of values is known		✔	✔	✔
"Counts," aka "Frequency of Distribution"	✔	✔	✔	✔
Mode	✔	✔	✔	✔
Median		✔	✔	✔
Mean			✔	✔
Can quantify the difference between each value			✔	✔
Can add or subtract values			✔	✔
Can multiple and divide values				✔
Has "true zero"				✔

Ratio

Ratio scales tell us about the order, they tell us the exact value between units, AND they also have an absolute zero–which allows for a wide range of both descriptive and inferential statistics to be applied. Good examples of ratio variables include height and weight.

In summary, **nominal** variables are used to "*name*," or label a series of values. **Ordinal** scales provide good information about the *order* of choices, such as in a customer satisfaction survey. **Interval** scales give us the order of values + the ability to quantify *the difference between each one*. Finally, **Ratio** scales gi-ve us the ultimate–order, interval values, plus the *ability to calculate ratios* since a "true zero" can be defined.

Chapter 10

Testing of Hypothesis

Data Analysis as discussed earlier consists of Descriptive analysis and inferential analysis. Further descriptive and causal analysis is unidimentional, bivariate and multivariate analysis whereas inferential statistics or analysis consists of estimation of parameter values and hypothesis testing.

Before proceeding to Hypothesis testing it is essential to discuss estimation of parameter values. For estimation of parameter values

Important terms we need to understand are

1. *Population*: All units in any field of inquiry constitute universe and all elementary units (on the basis of one characteristic or more) constitute population. Quit often, we do not find any difference between population and universe, and as such the two terms are taken as interchangeable. The population or universe can be *finite* or *infinite*. The population is said to be finite if it consists of a fixed number of elements so that it is possible to enumerate it in its totality. An infinite population is that population in which it is theoretically impossible to observe all the elements. Thus, in an infinite population the number of items is infinite i.e., we cannot have any idea about the total number of items.

2. *Sampling Frame:* The elementary units or the group or cluster of such units may form the basis of sampling process in which case they are called as sampling units. A list containing all such sampling units is known as sampling frame. Thus sampling frame consists of a list of items from which the sample is to be drawn.

3. *Sampling Design:* A sample design is a definite plan for obtaining a sample from the sampling frame. It refers to the technique or the procedure the researcher would adopt in selecting some sampling units from which inferences about the population is drawn. Sampling design is determined before any data are collected.

4. *Statistic(s) and Parameter(s):* A statistic is a characteristic of a sample, whereas a parameter is a characteristic of a population. Thus, when we work out certain measures such as mean, median, mode or the like ones from samples, then they are called statistic(s) for they describe the characteristics of a sample. But when such measures describe the characteristics of a population, they are known as parameter(s). For instance, the population mean is a parameter, whereas the sample mean (X) is a statistic.

5. *Sampling Error:* Sample surveys do imply the study of a small portion of the population and as such there would naturally be a certain amount of inaccuracy in the information collected. This inaccuracy may be termed as sampling error or error variance. As opposed to sampling errors, we may have non-sampling errors which may creep in during the process of collecting actual information and such errors occur in all surveys whether census or sample. We have no way to measure non-sampling errors. A measure of the random sampling error can be calculated for a given sample design and size and this measure is often called the precision of the sampling plan.

6. *Precision:* Precision is the range within which the population average (or other parameter) will lie in accordance with the reliability specified in the confidence level as a percentage of the estimate ± or as a numerical quantity. For instance, if the estimate is $ 4000 and the precision desired is ± 4%, then the true value will be no less than $ 3840 and no more than $ 4160. This is the range (3840 to 4160) within which the true answer should lie.

7. *Confidence Level and Significance Level:* The confidence level or reliability is the expected percentage of times that the actual value will fall within the stated precision limits. Thus, if we take a confidence level of 95%, then we mean that there are 95 chances in 100 (or .95 in 1) that the sample results represent the true condition

of the population within a specified precision range against 5 chances in 100 (or .05 in 1) that it does not. Precision is the range within which the answer may vary and still be acceptable; confidence level indicates the likelihood that the answer will fall within that range, and the significance level indicates the likelihood that the answer will fall outside that range. We can always remember that if the confidence level is 95%, then the significance level will be (100 − 95) i.e., 5%; if the confidence level is 99%, the significance level is (100 − 99) i.e., 1%, and so on.

8. *Sampling Distribution:* We are often concerned with sampling distribution in sampling analysis. If we take certain number of samples and for each sample compute various statistical measures such as mean, standard deviation, etc., then we can find that each sample may give its own value for the statistic under consideration. All such values of a particular statistic, say mean, together with their relative frequencies will constitute the sampling distribution of the particular statistic, say mean.

Accordingly, we can have sampling distribution of mean, or the sampling distribution of standard deviation or the sampling distribution of any other statistical measure. The significance of sampling distribution follows from the fact that the mean of a sampling distribution is the same as the mean of the universe. Thus, the mean of the sampling distribution can be taken as the mean of the universe.

Types of sampling distributions that are commonly used are –

- Sampling distribution of mean;
- Sampling distribution of proportion;
- Student's '*t*' distribution;
- *F* distribution; and
- Chi-square distribution.

   a. *Sampling Distribution of Mean* – Sampling distribution of mean refers to the probability distribution of all the possible means of random samples of a given size that we take from a population. If samples are taken from a normal population, the sampling distribution of mean would also be normal. But when sampling is from a population which is not normal (may be positively or negatively skewed), even then, as per the central limit theorem, the sampling distribution of mean tends quite closer to the normal distribution, provided the number of sample items is large i.e., more than 30.

b. *Sampling Distribution of Proportion* – Like sampling distribution of mean, we can as well have a sampling distribution of proportion. This happens in case of statistics of attributes. Assume that we have worked out the proportion of defective parts in large number of samples, each with say 100 items, that have been taken from an infinite population and plot a probability distribution of the said proportions, we obtain what is known as the sampling distribution of the said proportions, we obtain what is known as the sampling distribution of proportion.

c. *t-distribution* – When population standard deviation is not known and the sample is of a small size ($n < 30$), we use t distribution for the sampling distribution of mean. The t-distribution tables are available which give the critical values of t for different degrees of freedom at various levels of significance. The table value of t for given degrees of freedom at a certain level of significance is compared with the calculated value of t from the sample data, and if the latter is either equal to or exceeds, we infer that the null hypothesis cannot be accepted.

d. *F-test* – Tables have been prepared for F distribution that give critical values of F for various values of degrees of freedom for larger as well as smaller variances. The calculated value of F from the sample data is compared with the corresponding table value of F and if the former is equal to or exceeds the latter, then we infer that the null hypothesis of the variances being equal cannot be accepted.

e. *Chi- square distribution* – Chi-square distribution is encountered when we deal with collections of values that involve adding up squares. Variances of samples require us to add a collection of squared quantities and thus have distributions that are related to chi-square distribution. If we take each one of a collection of sample variances, divide them by the known population variance and multiply these quotients by $(n - 1)$, where n means the number of items in the sample, we shall obtain a chi-square distribution.

Chi-square distribution is not symmetrical and all the values are positive. One must know the degrees of freedom for using chi-square distribution. This distribution may also be used for judging the significance of difference between observed and expected frequencies and also as a test of goodness of fit.

Sampling Theory

Sampling theory is a study of relationships existing between a population and samples drawn from the population. Sampling theory is applicable only to random samples. For this purpose the population or a universe may be defined as an aggregate of items possessing a common trait or traits. In other words, a universe is the complete group of items about which knowledge is sought. The universe may be finite or infinite. finite universe is one which has a definite and certain number of items, but when the number of items is uncertain and infinite, the universe is said to be an infinite universe. Similarly, the universe may be hypothetical or existent. In the former case the universe in fact does not exist and we can only imagine the items constituting it. Tossing of a coin or throwing a dice are examples of hypothetical universe. Existent universe is a universe of concrete objects i.e., the universe where the items constituting it really exist. On the other hand, the term sample refers to that part of the universe which is selected for the purpose of investigation. The theory of sampling studies the relationships that exist between the universe and the sample or samples drawn from it.

The main problem of sampling theory is the problem of relationship between a parameter and a statistic. The theory of sampling is concerned with estimating the properties of the population from those of the sample and also with gauging the precision of the estimate. This sort of movement from particular (sample) towards general (universe) is what is known as statistical induction or statistical inference. In more clear terms "from the sample we attempt to draw inference concerning the universe. In order to be able to follow this inductive method, we first follow a deductive argument which is that we imagine a population or universe (finite or infinite) and investigate the behaviour of the samples drawn from this universe applying the laws of probability." The methodology dealing with all this is known as sampling theory.

The following are the primary objectives of sampling theory –

(i) Statistical estimation: Sampling theory helps in estimating unknown population parameters from a knowledge of statistical measures based on sample studies. In other words, **to obtain an estimate of parameter from statistic** is the main objective of the sampling theory. The estimate can either be a point estimate or it may be an interval estimate. Point estimate is a single estimate expressed in the form of a single figure, but interval estimate has two limits viz., the upper limit and the lower limit within which the parameter value may lie.

(ii) Testing of hypotheses: The second objective of sampling theory is to enable us to decide **whether to accept or reject hypothesis**; the sampling theory helps in determining whether observed differences are actually due to chance or whether they are really significant.

(iii) Statistical inference: Sampling theory helps in making **generalisation about the population/universe** from the studies based on samples drawn from it. It also helps in determining the accuracy of such generalisations.

The theory of sampling can be studied under two heads viz.,

a. The sampling of attributes and
b. The sampling of variables

in the context of large and small samples (By small sample is commonly understood any sample that includes 30 or fewer items, whereas a large sample is one in which the number of items is more than 30).

When we study some qualitative characteristic of the items in a population, we obtain statistics of attributes in the form of two classes;

one class consisting of items wherein the attribute is present and the other class consisting of items wherein the attribute is absent. The presence of an attribute may be termed as a 'success' and its absence a 'failure.' We generally consider the following three types of problems in case of sampling of attributes:

(i) The parameter value may be given and it is only to be tested if an observed 'statistic' is its estimate.

(ii) The parameter value is not known and we have to estimate it from the sample.

(iii) Examination of the reliability of the estimate i.e., the problem of finding out how far the estimate is expected to deviate from the true value for the population.

All the above stated problems are studied using the appropriate standard errors and the tests of Significance.

The theory of sampling can be applied in the context of statistics of variables (i.e., data relating to some characteristic concerning population which can be measured or enumerated with the help of some well defined statistical unit) in which case the objective happens to be : (i) to compare the observed and expected values and to find if the difference can be ascribed to the fluctuations of sampling; (ii) to estimate population parameters from the sample, and (iii) to find out the degree of reliability of the estimate.

The tests of significance used for dealing with problems relating to large samples are different from those used for small samples. This is so because the assumptions we make in case of large samples do not hold good for small samples. In case of large samples, we assume that the sampling distribution tends to be normal and the sample values are approximately close to the population values. As such we use the characteristics of normal distribution and apply what is known as z-test. When n is large, the probability of a sample value of the statistic deviating from the parameter by more than 3 times its standard error is very small (it is 0.0027 as per the table giving area under normal curve) and as such the z-test is applied to find out the degree of reliability of a statistic in case of large samples.

The sampling theory for large samples is not applicable in small samples because when samples are small, we cannot assume that the sampling distribution is approximately normal. As such we require a new technique for handlng small samples, particularly when population parameters are unknown. Sir William S. Gosset (pen name Student) developed a significance test, known as Student's *t*-test, based on *t* distribution and through it made significant contribution in the theory of sampling applicable in case of small samples.

Student's *t*-test is used when two conditions are fulfilled viz., the sample size is 30 or less and the population variance is not known. While using *t*-test we assume that the population from which sample has been taken is normal or approximately normal, sample is a random sample, observations are independent, there is no measurement error and that in the case of two samples when equality of the two population means is to be tested, we assume that the population variances are equal. For applying *t*-test, we work out the value of test statistic (i.e., '*t*') and then compare with the table value of *t* (based on '*t*' distribution) at certain level of significance for given degrees of freedom. If the calculated value of '*t*' is either equal to or exceeds the table value, we infer that the difference is significant, but if calculated value of *t* is less than the concerning table value of *t*, the difference is not treated as significant.

Hypothesis Testing

Decision-makers often face situations wherein they are interested in testing hypotheses on the basis of available information and then take decisions on the basis of such testing. In social science, where direct knowledge of population parameter(s) is rare, hypothesis testing is the often used strategy for deciding whether a sample data offer such support for a hypothesis that generalisation can be made. Thus hypothesis testing enables us to make probability statements about population parameter(s).

Some Basics of Hypothesis Testing

Hypothesis

A hypothesis may be defined as a proposition or a set of proposition set forth as an explanation for the occurrence of some specified group of phenomena either asserted merely as a provisional conjecture to guide some investigation or accepted as highly probable in the light of established facts.

A research hypothesis is a predictive statement, capable of being tested by scientific methods, that relates an independent variable to some dependent variable.

Example: Method A of performing an activity is better than method B

Students undergoing practical training along with regular class perform better in exam.

Basic Characteristics of Hypothesis

(i) Hypothesis should be clear and precise.

(ii) Hypothesis should be capable of being tested.

(iii) Hypothesis should state relationship between variables, if it happens to be a relational hypothesis.

(iv) Hypothesis should be limited in scope and must be specific.

(v) Hypothesis should be stated as far as possible in most simple terms so that the same is easily understandable by all concerned.

(vi) Hypothesis should be consistent with most known facts i.e., it must be consistent with a substantial body of established facts.

(vii) Hypothesis should be amenable to testing within a reasonable time.

(viii) Hypothesis must explain the facts that gave rise to the need for explanation.

Null Hypothesis and Alternative Hypothesis

In the context of statistical analysis, we often talk about null hypothesis and alternative hypothesis. If we are to compare method *A* with method *B* about its superiority and if we proceed on the assumption that both methods are equally good, then this assumption is termed as the null hypothesis. As against this, we may think that the method *A* is superior or the method *B* is inferior, we are then stating what is termed as alternative hypothesis. The null hypothesis is generally symbolized as H_0 and the alternative hypothesis as H_a.

Null Hypothesis is what you want to test and alternative hypothesis is opposite of null hypothesis.

If you state null hypothesis as mean value = 30 marks in a class test then,

Alternative hypothesis is Mean value ≠ 30

If we use = or ≠ sign, it is a two tailed test whereas if you use < or > sign it is a one tailed test

A null hypothesis may be rejected, but it can never be accepted based on a single test. A statistical test can have one of two outcomes: that the null hypothesis is rejected and the alternative hypothesis accepted, or that the null hypothesis is not rejected based on the evidence. It would be incorrect, however, to conclude that since the null hypothesis is not rejected, it can be accepted as valid. In classical hypothesis testing, there is no way to determine whether the null hypothesis is true.

Confidence Level and Significance Level

Confidence level is the confidence that out of 100 samples(n) a particular number (x)95 samples will be equal to sample mean...In fact the most common confidence level is 95% or 0.95 confidence level

Significance level is 1 - confidence level or 1 – 0.95 = 0.05 or 5% significance level

Similarly we may have 0.1, 0.01 or 0.05 significance levels

Confidence level + Significance level = 1

Testing of Hypothesis

Before discussing testing of Hypothesis it is essential to know more about Normal distribution.

Normal distribution has 4 properties

1. It is a bell shaped curve
2. Mean, median and mode lie at the centre of the curve
3. Mean divides the curve into two equal parts. Normal distribution is based on probability therefore equals to 1
4. It has two tails which do not touch the origin

This is how a normal distribution curve looks like

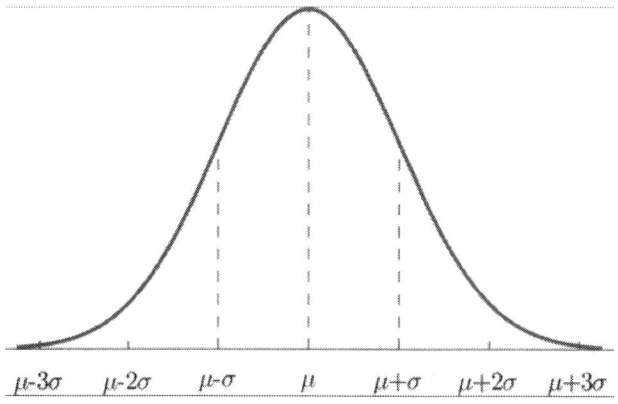

We use normal distribution for hypothesis testing

$$Z = \frac{X - \mu}{\sigma}$$

Z = z distribution

μ = Population mean

σ = Standard deviation

Since population mean cannot be used in all situations sample mean is used.

Sample mean = $\bar{X}$

In "Z" test population mean is used where as sample mean is used in a "t" test

Therefore,

$$t = \frac{X - \bar{X}}{\sigma/\sqrt{n}}$$

$\bar{X}$ = sample mean

n = sample size

σ = Standard deviation both "t" and "z" test are used for hypothesis testing.

Point to remember at this time is that where the distribution is normal, "z" and "t" tests are possible. If the distribution does not follow normal distribution then we need to used non parametric methods.

Before performing "z" test or "t" test. 2 tailed and 1 tailed concepts need to be understood.

If we look at the normal distribution curve, we observe two tails . To understand two tailed and one tailed concepts it is necessary to know critical values and calculated values

- Critical values are derived from 'z' and 't' tables. These are also called as tabulated values
- Calculated values are those derived from formulas

$$z = \frac{X-\mu}{\sigma} \quad \text{or} \quad t = \frac{X - \bar{X}}{\sigma/\sqrt{n}}$$

If a distribution has two critical values, one +ve and one –ve, it is a two tailed test. Whereas if only one critical value exists it is one tailed test.

Acceptance and rejection regions in case of one tailed test (left-tail) with 5% significance

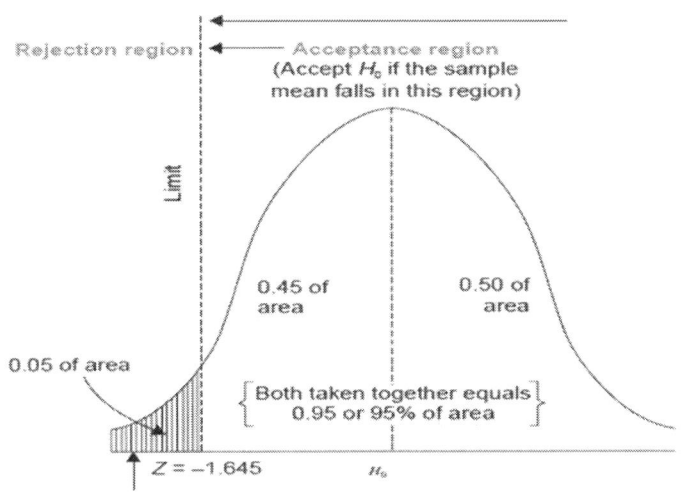

Acceptance and rejection regions in case of one

tailed test (right-tail) with 5% significance

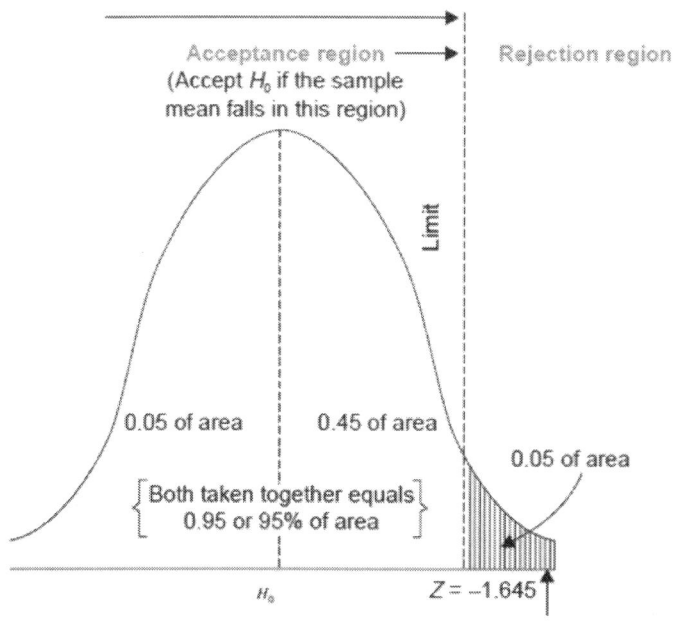

Further,

2 tailed test has

    2 acceptance regions

    2 critical points

    2 rejection regions

1 tailed (positive/right tail) has

    1 acceptance region

    1 critical point

    1 rejection region

1 tailed (negative/left tail) has

    1 acceptance region

    1 critical point

    1 rejection region

Now restating Null and alternative hypothesis, let us assume that

Null hypothesis states that mean value = 30

Alternative hypothesis states that mean value ≠ 30

If we use = or ≠ sign then it is a two tailed test whereas if we use < or > sign then it is one tailed test.

>implies positive critical values and < negative critical values

If calculated 'z' or 't' value lies in acceptance region then null hypothesis is accepted otherwise alternative hypothesis is accepted.

If 'z' or 't' calculated lies in the acceptance region, then accept null hypotheses

If 'z' or 't' calculated lies in the rejection region then accept alternative hypothesis

Point to note:

SPSS (Statistical Package for Social Sciences) does not consider 'z' and 't' values but only 'p' value (there are a number of statistical packages such as SPSS, STATA, E-Views etc., available for carrying out data analysis. In this section there are references to data analysis using SPSS. For further clarity, the reader is advised to refer to SPSS survival manuals)

P value rules

If 'p' value is < significance level (0.05) reject null hypothesis and accept alternative hypothesis

If 'p' value is > significance level (0.05) accept null hypothesis and reject alternative hypothesis

Every test of SPSS is based on p values and

f p < sig (accept alternative hypothesis)

If p > sig (accept null hypothesis)

Therefore, **finally** the following steps are involved in hypothesis testing–

1. Formulate the null hypothesis $H0$ and the alternative hypothesis $H1$.
2. Select an appropriate statistical technique and the corresponding test statistic.
3. Choose the level of significance, α.

4. Determine the sample size and collect the data. Calculate the value of the test statistic.
5. Determine the probability associated with the test statistic under the null hypothesis, using the sampling distribution of the test statistic. Alternatively, determine the critical values associated with the test statistic that divide the rejection and non-rejection region.
6. Compare the probability associated with the test statistic with the level of significance specified. Alternatively, determine whether the test statistic has fallen into the rejection or the non-rejection region.
7. Make the statistical decision to reject or not reject the null hypothesis.
8. Express the statistical decision in terms of the research problem.

How to Choose a Suitable Statistic

Most statistics and research methodology courses tell you how to calculate different statistics but fail to teach how to choose the statistical method that is most suitable to your research. The approach followed by in SPSS survival manuals is found quiet appropriate in selecting the suitable statistic. Accordingly there are different techniques used to explore the *relationship among variables and* techniques when you want to explore the *differences between groups.*

For Exploring Relationships among Variables

Most often when you conduct a survey research you will not be interested in differences between groups, but instead in the strength of the relationship between variables. There are a number of different techniques that you can use. These are summarized as follows

Pearson Correlation – Pearson correlation is used when you want to explore the strength of the relationship between two continuous variables. This gives you an indication of both the direction (positive or negative) and the strength of the relationship. A positive correlation indicates that as one variable increases, so does the other. A negative correlation indicates that as one variable increases, the other decreases.

Correlation is used when you wish to describe the strength and direction of the relationship between two variables (usually continuous). It can also be used when one of the variables is dichotomous—that is, it has only two values (e.g. sex: males/females). The statistic obtained is Pearson's product-moment correlation (r).

Partial Correlation – Partial correlation is an extension of Pearson correlation—it allows you to control for the possible effects of another confounding variable. Partial correlation 'removes' the effect of the confounding variable (e.g. socially desirable responding), allowing you to get a more accurate picture of the relationship between your two variables of interest.

Partial correlation is used when you wish to explore the relationship between two variables while statistically controlling for a third variable. This is useful when you suspect that the relationship between your two variables of interest may be influenced, or confounded, by the impact of a third variable. Partial correlation statistically removes the influence of the third variable, giving a cleaner picture of the actual relationship between your two variables.

Multiple Regression – Multiple regression is a more sophisticated extension of correlation and is used when you want to explore the predictive ability of a set of independent variables on one *continuous* dependent measure. Different types of multiple regression allow you to compare the predictive ability of particular independent variables and to find the best set of variables to predict a dependent variable.

Multiple regression allows prediction of a single dependent continuous variable from a group of independent variables. It can be used to test the predictive power of a set of variables and to assess the relative contribution of each individual variable.

Logistic regression is used instead of multiple regression when your dependent variable is categorical. It can be used to test the predictive power of a set of variables and to assess the relative contribution of each individual variable.

Factor Analysis – Factor analysis allows you to condense a large set of variables or scale items down to a smaller, more manageable number of dimensions or factors. It does this by summarizing the underlying patterns of correlation and looking for 'clumps' or groups of closely related items. This technique is often used when developing scales and measures, to identify the underlying structure.

Factor analysis is used when you have a large number of related variables (e.g. the items that make up a scale), and you wish to explore the underlying structure of this set of variables. It is useful in reducing a large number of related variables to a smaller, more manageable, number of dimensions or components.

All of the analyses described above involve exploration of the relationship between continuous variables. If you have only categorical variables, you can use the chisquare test for relatedness or independence to explore their relationship (e.g. if you wanted to see whether gender influenced clients' dropout rates from a treatment program). In this situation you are interested in the number of people in each category (males and females, who drop out of/complete the program), rather than their score on a scale.

Some Other Analysis

Discriminant Function Analysis is used when you want to explore the predictive ability of a set of independent variables, on one categorical dependent measure. That is, you want to know which variables best predict group membership. The dependent variable in this case is usually some clear criterion (passed/failed, dropped out of/continued with treatment).

Canonical Correlation is used when you wish to analyse the relationship between two sets of variables. For example, a researcher might be interested in how a variety of demographic variables relate to measures of wellbeing and adjustment.

Structural Equation Modelling is a relatively new, and quite sophisticated, technique that allows you to test various models concerning the interrelationships among a set of variables.

Based on multiple regression and factor analytic techniques, it allows you to evaluate the importance of each of the independent variables in the model and to test the overall fit of the model to your data. It also allows you to compare alternative models. SPSS does not have a structural equation modelling module, but it does support an 'add on' called AMOS.

Exploring Differences between Groups

There is another set of statistics that can be used when you want to find out whether there is a statistically significant difference among a number of groups. Most of these analyses involve comparing the mean score for each group on one or more dependent variables. There are a number of different but related statistics in this group. The main techniques are very briefly described below.

T-tests

T-tests are used when you have *two* groups (e.g. males and females) or two sets of data (before and after), and you wish to compare the mean score on some continuous variable. There are two main types of t-tests. Paired sample t-tests (also called repeated measures) are used when you are interested in changes in scores for subjects tested at Time 1, and then again at Time 2 (often after some intervention or event). The samples are 'related' because they are the *same* people tested each time. Independent sample t-tests are used when you have two *different* (independent) groups of people (males and females), and you are interested in comparing their scores. In this case you collect information on only one occasion, but from two different sets of people.

One-Way Analysis of Variance

One-way analysis of variance is similar to a t-test, but is used when you have *two or more groups* and you wish to compare their mean scores on a continuous variable. It is called one-way because you are looking at the impact of only one independent variable on your dependent variable. A one-way analysis of variance (ANOVA) will let you know whether your groups differ, but it won't tell you where the significant difference is (gp1/gp3, gp2/gp3 etc.). You can conduct posthoc comparisons to find out which groups are significantly different from one another. You could also choose to test differences between specific groups, rather than comparing all the groups, by using planned comparisons. Similar to t-tests.

There are two types of one-way ANOVAs: repeated measures ANOVA (same people on more than two occasions), and between-groups (or independent samples) ANOVA, where you are comparing the mean scores of two or more different groups of people.

Two-way analysis of variance -Two-way analysis of variance allows you to test the impact of two independent variables on one dependent variable. The advantage of using a two-way ANOVA is that it allows you to test for an interaction effect—that is, when the effect of one independent variable is influenced by another; for example, when you suspect that optimism increases with age, but only for males. It also tests for 'main effects'—that is, the overall effect of each independent variable (e.g. sex, age).

There are two different two-way ANOVAs: between-groups ANOVA (when the groups are different) and repeated measures ANOVA (when the same people are tested on more than one occasion). Some research designs combine both between groups and repeated measures in the one study. These are referred to as 'Mixed Between-Within Designs,' or 'Split Plot.'

Multivariate Analysis of Variance

Multivariate analysis of variance (MANOVA) is used when you want to compare your groups on a number of different, but *related*, dependent variables: for example, comparing the effects of different treatments on a variety of outcome measures (e.g. anxiety, depression, physical symptoms). Multivariate ANOVA can be used with one-way, two-way and higher factorial designs involving one, two, or more independent variables.

Analysis of Covariance

Analysis of covariance (ANCOVA) is used when you want to statistically control for the possible effects of an additional confounding variable (covariate). This is useful when you suspect that your groups differ on some variable that may influence the effect that your independent variables have on your dependent variable. To be sure that it is the independent variable that is doing the influencing, ANCOVA statistically removes the effect of the covariate. Analysis of covariance can be used as part of a one-way, two-way or multivariate design.

Further Hypothesis testing may also be studied in terms of parametric analysis and non parametric analysis.

Parametric statistical analysis may be employed effectively in the following conditions:

1. Probability or representative sample has been employed in the investigation.
2. Variables of the study can be qualified at interval scale.
3. Specific assumptions are fulfilled. The obtained data are normally distributed or not free distribution.
4. The population of the study has been clearly defined.
5. Objectives of the research study are clearly defined.

Whereas, Non parametric statistical analysis may be used effectively in the following situations:

1. When non-probability sample is selected in the research study.
2. The variables of the study are quantified at any level of measurement, mainly, nominal and ordinal scale. It may be in the discrete form.
3. No assumption is required for this approach.
4. Free distribution of data, may be skewed or may be normally distributed.

The important parametric tests are: (1) z-test; (2) t-test; (3) χ^2-test, and (4) F-test. All these tests are based on the assumption of normality i.e., the source of data is considered to be normally distributed.

In some cases the population may not be normally distributed, yet the tests will be applicable on account of the fact that we mostly deal with samples and the sampling distributions closely approach normal distributions.

z-test is based on the normal probability distribution and is used for judging the significance of several statistical measures, particularly the mean. The relevant test statistic, z, is worked out and compared with its probable value (to be read from table showing area under normal curve) at a specified level of significance for judging the significance of the measure concerned. This is a most frequently used test in research studies. This test is used even when binomial distribution or t-distribution is applicable on the presumption that such a distribution tends to approximate normal distribution as 'n' becomes larger.

z-test is generally used for comparing the mean of a sample to some hypothesised mean for the population in case of large sample, or when population variance is known. z-test is also used for judging he significance of difference between means of two independent samples in case of large samples, or when population variance is known. z-test is also used for comparing the sample proportion to a theoretical value of population proportion or for judging the difference in proportions of two independent samples when n happens to be large. Besides, this test may be used for judging the significance of median, mode, coefficient of correlation and several other measures.

t-test is based on t-distribution and is considered an appropriate test for judging the significance of a sample mean or for judging the significance of difference between the means of two samples in case of small sample(s) when population variance is not known (in which case we use variance of the sample as an estimate of the population variance).

In case two samples are related, we use **paired t-test** (or what is known as difference test) for judging the significance of the mean of difference between the two related samples. It can also be used for judging the significance of the coefficients of simple and partial correlations. The relevant test statistic, t, is calculated from the sample data and then compared with its probable value based on t-distribution (to be read from the table that gives probable values of t for different levels of significance for different degrees of freedom) at a specified level of significance for concerning degrees of freedom for accepting or rejecting the null hypothesis. It may be noted that t-test applies only in case of small sample(s) when population variance is unknown.

χ^2-test is based on chi-square distribution and as a parametric test is used for comparing a sample variance to a theoretical population variance. **χ^2 - test is also used as a test of goodness of fit and also as a test of independence in which case it is a non-parametric test.**

F-test is based on F-distribution and is used to compare the variance of the two-independent samples. This test is also used in the context of analysis of variance (ANOVA) for judging the significance of more than two sample means at one and the same time. It is also used for judging the significance of multiple correlation coefficients. Test statistic, F, is calculated and compared with its probable value (to be seen in the F-ratio tables for different degrees of freedom for greater and smaller variances at specified level of significance) for accepting or rejecting the null hypothesis.

In a statistical test, two kinds of assertions are involved viz., an assertion directly related to the purpose of investigation and other assertions to make a probability statement. The former is an assertion to be tested and is technically called a hypothesis, whereas the set of all other assertions is called the model. When we apply a test (to test the hypothesis) without a model, it is known as distribution-free test, or the nonparametric test. Non-parametric tests do not make an assumption about the parameters of the population and thus do not make use of the parameters of the distribution.

In other words, under non-parametric or distribution-free tests we do not assume that a particular distribution is applicable, or that a certain value is attached to a parameter of the population

Tests of hypotheses with 'order statistics' or 'nonparametric statistics' or 'distribution-free' statistics are known as nonparametric or distribution-free tests. The following distribution-free tests are important and generally used:

a. Test of a hypothesis concerning some single value for the given data (such as one-sample sign test).

b. Test of a hypothesis concerning no difference among two or more sets of data (such as two-sample sign test, Fisher-Irwin test, Rank sum test, etc.)

c. Test of a hypothesis of a relationship between variables (such as Rank correlation, *Kendall's coefficient of concordance* and other tests for dependence.

d. Test of a hypothesis concerning variation in the given data i.e., test analogous to ANOVA viz., Kruskal-Wallis test.

e. Tests of randomness of a sample based on the theory of runs viz., one sample runs test.

f. Test of hypothesis to determine if categorical data shows dependency or if two classifications are independent viz., the chi-square test. The chi-square test can as well be used to make comparison between theoretical populations and actual data when categories are used.

While using SPSS the Non-parametric technique and Parametric alternative available are as follows:

Non-parametric technique	Parametric alternative available
Chi-square for independence	None
Mann-Whitney Test	Independent-samples t-test
Wilcoxon Signed Rank Test	Paired-samples t-test
Kruskal-Wallis Test	One-way between-groups ANOVA
Friedman Test	One-way repeated-measures ANOVA
Spearman Rank Order Correlation	Pearson's product-moment correlation

Decision Making in Choosing the Right Statistics for Your Study

Before the researcher chooses the right statistic for his study he need to consider various aspects of the research such as the type of question you wish to address, the type of items and scales that were included in your questionnaire, the nature of the data you have available for each of your variables and the assumptions that must be met for each of the different statistical techniques.

Chapter 11

Report Writing

Research report is considered a major component of the research study and the research task remains incomplete until a report is prepared. Writing of report is the last step in a research study and requires a set of skills somewhat different from those called for in respect of the earlier stages of research. This task should be accomplished by the researcher with utmost care; he may seek the assistance and guidance of experts for the purpose.

The importance of a research study is to evaluate both scholastically and practically the contents of the written proposal and report of the study. The merit of the problem and its adequacy is examined on the basis of research proposal and the contribution of the study is judged on the basis of research report of thesis of the study. There are various formats of research report a researcher must understand its meaning and purpose. The following are the major writings formats of research work.

1. **Research Proposal or synopsis or outline of a research work or project.**
2. **Research Report or thesis**
3. **Research Summary, and**
4. **Research Abstracts.**

A research proposal deals with problem or topic that is to be investigated. It has a variety of formats which vary in their length. Writing a research proposal or synopsis includes an introductory section: problem hypotheses objectives, assumptions, method of study tools, justification and implications of the study. It is written in present or future tense. It covers four to ten pages. It is submitted for the final approval before starting the actual research work. The preparation of research proposal is significant in the development and pursuit of a research project. It is planning phase of a research work which is produced in the written form to judge its worth.

A research report deals with results of completed research work. After completing a research work, it is generally produced in the written form, and is called research report or thesis. A detailed description of research activities are provided in it. It has a variety of formats and vary as to its length. It is written in past tense and in third person. It is the final form of the research work. A research report includes usually the following chapters- Introductory or theoretical background, Review of related literature, Methodology, Data collection, Analysis of data, Discussion of results and findings of the study, Bibliography and Appendices. It is also submitted for evaluating its contributions. It serves the purpose of communicating the results of a research work done.

A research summary is the condensed version of research report. It provides the important aspects of research report or thesis. The purpose of the summary is to facilitate the readers or other scholars to understand about work done at a glance because to go through a research report it is very time consuming and difficult. Therefore, the main features of research report are summarized. It takes the form of research journal article or paper. It is also written in the past tense and covers six to twelve pages.

A research abstract is the condensed version of research summary. The main essence of the research work when reduced to a page or para is called research abstract. It includes title, method, sample and findings of the study. These abstracts are published in the journal as Abstracts.

The Research Report

The writing of research report is usually the concluding task of the research endeavour. Since the written report is an account of research project, the organization of the report follows quite closely the organization of the research project. The writing of the report is usually associated with the close of the research for project, few portions of writing may be done while the research study is in progress. It is also known as thesis or dissertation.

General Format of Research Report

A written format of a research work is known as thesis or research report. All types of research reports are expected to follow a general uniform, common pattern of format, style and structure. The general format of research report is evolved and it has become a tradition in academic area. A research report or thesis is an organized format of research work done. It is viewed in three major categories:

- A. Preliminaries,
- B. Textual Body, and
- C. References.

Each category has been outlined further as follows:

A. Preliminary Section

1. Title page
2. Preface or acknowledgements
3. Table of content
4. List of tables (if any)
5. List of figures (if any).

B. Main Body of Report or Textual Body

1. Introduction
    - (a) Statement of the problem
    - (b) Objectives of the study
    - (c) Hypotheses to be tested
    - (d) Significance of the problem
    - (e) Assumptions and delimitations.
    - (f) Definitions of Important terms used.
2. Review of related literature.
3. Design of the study
    - (a) Method and procedure used
    - (b) Tools of research or sources of data

(c) Techniques of data collection

   (d) Description of techniques used.

   4. Analysis and presentation of data

      (a) Analysis of data

      (b) Tables and interpretation

      (c) Figures and interpretation.

   5. Conclusions

      (a) Discussion of results

      (b) Main Findings and inferences

      (c) Implication of the findings and limitations

      (d) Suggestions for further studies.

C. Reference Section

1. Bibliography
2. Appendices (if any)
3. Index or glossary (if any).

The detailed explanation of each aspect is given here

(A) Preliminary Section

As the preliminaries form a significant part of the whole thesis report, due care should be taken in preparing them. If the specifications are already laid down by some colleges or universities they shouldbbe observed. However, a general standard pattern suggested here in each case will be helpful for a researcher.

1. Title Page

This is the first page of a thesis or a dissertation. It includes:

(a) Title of thesis.

(b) Name of the candidate.

(c) Purpose or relationship of the thesis to the course or degree requirement.

(d) College and/or department in which the candidate has been admitted for the degree.

(e) Name of the university to which it is submitted.

(f) Month and year of submission or acceptance.

The title should be accurate, concise and clearly printed in capital letters. It should convey the main theme of the problem investigated and if possible one should give a clue about the method or type of research involved..

2. Preface or Acknowledgement

A preface is different from introduction. It is a brief account of the purport or the origin and the utility of the study for which the thesis is presented. It also includes the acknowledgement to the persons and sources that have been helpful to the investigator. If the researcher does not want to mention anything about the study on this page except acknowledging debt to others, it will be desirable to use the title simple and restrained without flattery and effusive recognition for help by the family members and others. The preface should not be too long with too many details about the research work or its organization, which can appear in introduction. The word PREFACE or ACKNOWLEDGEMENT should be typed in capital letters. It should be written in an impressive way.

3. Table of Contents

This section lists all the main chapter headings and the essential sub-heading in each with the appropriate page numbers against each. The listing of main chapters is generally preceded by some preliminaries like preface or acknowledgement, list of tables, list of figures, abstract or synopsis and their respective pages in small Roman numbers and followed at the end by appendices, and Indexes.

Contents should neither be too detailed nor too sketchy the table of contents should serve an important purpose in providing an outline of the contents of the report. The capitalized title 'Contents' should be the central heading of the page and the capitalized word 'CHAPTER' and 'PAGE' should lead to the numbers of chapters and those of pages respectively on the left and right margins.

4. List of Tables

The table of contents is followed by the list of tables on a separate page. This list of tables consists of the titles or captions of the tables included in the thesis along with the page number where these can be located.

The capitalized title 'LIST OF TABLES' should be the central heading of the page and the capital words 'TABLE' and 'PAGE' should lead to the numbers and those of pages respectively at left and right margins.

5. List of Figures and Illustrations

If any charts graphs or any other illustrations are used in the thesis, a list of figures on a separate page is prepared in the same form as the list of tables except that they are numbered with Arabic numbers.

Example-

Table of Contents

CONTENTS

Preface

List of Tables

List of Figures

I. INTRODUCTION

(*a*) Statement of Problem

(*b*) Objectives

(*c*) Hypotheses

(*d*) Assumptions and Limitations

II. REVIEW OF LITERATURE

III. DESIGN OF RESEARCH

(*a*) Method of Sample

(*b*) Procedure and Technique

(*c*) Statistical Technique

IV. ANALYSIS OF DATA

V. CONCLUSIONS

Bibliography

Appendix

LIST OF TABLES

Table	Page
1. SampleStructure	20
2. Distribution of Academic Qualification	22
3. Distribution of Aptitude Scores	23
4. Regression Weights	28

Similarly list-of figures is prepared. The page number of figures is given facing the page number of the report.

(B) Main Body of Report or Textual Body

The text of the thesis is the most important section in the organization of research report. The quality of worth of thesis is mainly examined. It is the original production of the researcher. The report of the main body serves the function of demonstrating the competence of the researcher. If any sentence, paragraph, concept fails to serve the single function within a given section or chapter, it is irrelevant The subject matter of any chapter should be relevant to that point. Generally the main body of the research reports consists of five or six chapters.

Chapter

I. Introduction or Theoretical Frame Work

II. Review of Related Literature

III. Design or Methodology

IV. Analysis and Interpretation of Data.

V. Conclusions and Suggestions for the Further Researches.

Chapter 1. Introduction or Theoretical Frame Work

The main purpose of this chapter is to indicate the need and scope of the study. It consists essentially of the statement of research inquiry. It is reported in past tense form of work completed. The problem objectives, hypotheses, assumptions and delimitations of the study are reported precisely. If an introduction is required, the researcher should make certain that it is an introduction that generates an interest and appropriate mental set which introductions are regarded as capable of producing. It must be long enough to do its jobs and nothing more.

Chapter 2. Review of Related Literature

This chapter is essential in most of the research studies. It presents the comprehensive development of the problem background. It Indicates what has already been studied by others, which has a bearing upon the present study. The review of literature stresses two aspects: the first is the consideration of the subject-matter and it is likely more important than the other. The second is related to methodology and design. The review chapter is devoted to the development of the problem statement or the object of the inquiry. The review is utilized to retain a direct relevancy to the study in hand. It is the balancing chapter of the research report.

Chapter 3. Design or Methodology of Research

This chapter indicates the line of approach of the study. The first aspect deals with the method, population and sample of the study and second part provides the tools and techniques employed in the research. It also presents the procedure of the study. The whole plan of the study is discussed in detail under this chapter.

Administration of tools and scoring procedure are reported systematically. The data organization and presentation should be given in this section. It may be reported in a separate chapter of the report.

Chapter 4. Analysis and Interpretation of the Data

In this chapter analysis and results are reported so as to draw the inferences of the study. The analysis of data are presented in tabular form and in figures or pictorial presentation. The results are interpreted at length. This chapter provides the original work or contribution by the researcher. The communicative accuracy is required in this chapter. The text must be developed to ensure an effective ordering of the evidences.

Chapter 5. Conclusions and Suggestions

This is most important chapter of the report. It requires the creative and reflective aspect of the researcher. The results are discussed to make them more meaningful comparison of the results with the evidence in the review section should be woven into the text whenever such a discussion can serve to clarify the points being reported. This is the final chapter of a report, thus findings of the study are summarized and suggestions for the further studies are also given. The implications and delimitations of the findings are also mentioned in this section. The main thrust in the section is the answer of the question or solution of the problem. The validity of the findings should be mentioned.

(C) Reference Section

This is the third section of a research report. It consists of generally the bibliography and appendices. It is also essential to include glossary and index for the convenience of the readers. The bibliography, appendix, glossary and index all these are written on a separate page - in the centre with capital letters.

1. Bibliography

The bibliography is a list of the printed sources utilized in the research work. The publications used for information-yield but not quoted in the report may also be included in the bibliography. The format of the bibliography depend on the footnote style. If the foot-notes reference in the text are numbered to refer to the source in the bibliography, the entries must be numerically listed in the order of appearance in the text. The various format manuals include information on form for the bibliography. If the list of sources is too large the bibliography should be categorized in the following sections: Books, monographs, documents and reports, periodicals and journals, essay and articles, unpublished thesis and material and newspapers.

If selected sources are reported the words 'Selected Bibliography' should be written. In writing bibliography the surname is written first than initials, year of publication, title of the book, publishers name, place and total number of pages. The following are the examples of writing bibliography:

(*i*) Example for single author:

Best, John. W (1977) 'Research in Education,' 3rd ed., New Jersy : Prentice-Hall Inc. Englewood Cliffs, 403 pp.

(*ii*) Example for two authors: The only difference is that second author's name is written differently i.e. initial first and surname at the end in a usual manner.

McGrath, J.H. and D. Gene Watts on (1970) 'Research Methods and Designs for Education' Pennsylvania: International Text-Book Company, 222 pp.

(*iii*) Example for three or more authors:

Selltiz, Claire et al. (1959) "Research Method in Social Relations," New York: Holt, Rinehart and Winston, 424 pp.

(*iv*) Example for editor as author:

Buros, Oscar K. ed. (1965) 'The Sixth Mental Measurement,' Yearbook: Highland Park, N.J. : Gryphon Press 1163 pp.

(*v*) Example for author not given:

Author's Guide (1955) Englewood Cliffs, N.J. Prentice Hall, 121 pp.

(*vi*) Example for publication of an association, Agency or Society:

National Society for the study of Education (1955), 'Modern Philosophies of Education' 54th Yearbook, Part-I, The University of Chicago Press, Chicago 37 pp.

Or

'Modern Philosophies of Education' (1955), National Society for the Study of Education, 54th Yearbook Part-I, Chicago: The Chicago University Press 374 pp.

(*vii*) Example for unpublished thesis:

Sharma, R.A. (1972), 'Some Predictors of Teacher Effectiveness' Unpublished Ph.D. Thesis Submitted to AASTU University, 320 pp.

(*viii*) Article in an Encyclopaedia and Hand Book.

Barr, A.S. (1944), 'Criteria of Teacher-Effectiveness' Ebel's Encyclopaedia of Educational Research, 742 p. Smith, B.O. (1964),

'Relationship of Teaching and Learning,' Gage, Hand Book of Research in Teaching, 426 p.

(*ix*) Example for Journals and Periodicals:

Bar, A.S. (1940), 'The Measurement and Prediction of Teaching Efficiency,' Review of Educational Research, Vol. 10, No. 4, pp. 185-190.

Leeds, C.H. (1969), Predictive Validity of MTAII,' The Journal of Teacher Education, Vol. 20 NO.1.

(*x*) A chapter written by an author other than the editor:

Maccoby E.E. (1954), "The Interview: A Tool of Social Science," Chapter 12, in the Hand Book of Social Psychology, Addison, Wesley Cambridge Mass.

(*xi*) Quotations primary source cannot be located:

Kelley, E.P. (1950), 'Education for what is Real,' As cited by Edward A. Krug, 'Curriculum Planning,' New York: Harper and Row Publishers, 55 pp.

The place of publication may be written before the home of publishers e.g. New York: Harper and Row Publishers, 55 pp.

2. Appendix

An appendix is the important reference materials category. It includes the material which can not be logically included in the main body or textual body of the research report or the relevant materials too unwieldy to include in the main body. The appendix usually includes: tools of research, statistical tables and sometime raw-data (when data were processed through computer). Even the material of minor importance e.g. forms, letters, reminders, interview sheets, blank questionnaires, charts, tables, lengthy questions, report of cases (if follow-up or case studies have been conducted). The tools and other material should be placed first and tables at the end and page numbers should be assigned in Roman Numbers (i, ii, xxi). The appendix serves the function of providing greater clarity and authenticity for the readers or consumers of the thesis. The items of the appendix are very essential for a good research report.

3. Index and Glossary

When a research report is published in index, must be given. The index includes authors and subjects and topics or words in alphabetical order. In the report glossary should be provided. It includes the meanings or definitions of some words and terms used in the research report. Some notations symbols or abbreviations should be explained what actually they mean or indicate in the study.

Mechanics of Report Writing

A research report writing is a highly technical activity. It includes various mechanics for a smooth flow of the thesis. The mechanical aspect has been standardized which must be followed by researcher in preparing a thesis. Such mechanics involve the following issues:

(a) Footnotes and references,

(b) Style of writing,

(c) Headings,

(d) Tables,

(e) Figures,

(f) Pagination,

(g) Proof reading, and

(h) Binding and submission.

(a) Footnotes

Sometimes it is desirable to quote some authoritative views or statements from written works of others in the research report. It may be necessary from various purposes viz. to review the related literature, to support to give the rationale for one's viewpoint. Each quotation must have a footnote or reference indicating the sources from which it is borrowed. All these sources and authority be acknowledged both for intellectual honesty and for validity of one's research.

The footnotes are placed at the bottom of the page and are separated from the text by a three cms horizontal line drawn from the left margin. Footnotes are numbered consecutively within a chapter.

Ibid–In consecutive reference to the same work the Latin abbreviation Ibid (Indicates same page as earlier footnote), Ibid p. 36 (same work, but a different page 36) is used.

(b) Style of Preparing Thesis

The research report should be written in a style that it is creative, clear and concise. Therefore the following considerations should be kept in view in writing a research report.

1. The research must be reported in full and its results are subjected to criticism and verification.
2. A research report is always written in third person i.e. he, she or the investigator. I, we, you, my, our and us should not be used.
3. It is prepared and written in past tense and present-prefect tense because it is reported usually after completion of the work.
4. The scientific language is used rather than literary language. The British-English pattern is followed in writing a research report. The spellings of the words are employed of the British English.
5. It is typed printed/cyclostyled on 11" 9" size (thesis size) sunlit bond papers. There should be left a margin of 1-1/2" right margin one inch top and bottom margin should be 1-1/4" in each. The same machine of typing must be used for typing research report.
6. The presentation of matter should be in floating sequence. There should be consistency in the form and content organization.
7. An appropriate and proper format of research report should be used.
8. The footnotes, references, tables, figures, heading, subheading and bibliography should be provided in its standard form.
9. It should be typed in double space, quotations or citation should be given in single space. A word should not be split in two aspects due to the shortage of space in a line. A table, figure and diagram should always be given on a single pace. If table size is large. a large size paper should be used. It should not continue on the next page.

10. A typist with great experience and proficiency should be employed for preparing thesis or dissertation, because it is the responsibility of the researcher that a thesis should be typed in proper form. The correction of major errors is not the responsibility of the typist.

11. Good research reports are not written hurriedly. Even an expert and experienced researcher revises many times before he submits a manuscript for typing. Typographical standards for the thesis or dissertation are more exacting. Therefore, every typist cannot prepare a thesis, there are the experts for typing thesis, who should be employed for typing thesis.

(c) Headings

Generally a research report is divided into chapters, each chapter begins from a new page. The title of a chapter is called the chapter heading. The work 'CHAPTER' is written in capital letters, in the centre of the page and title is placed three spaces of the chapter.

(d) Tables

A table is used for presenting statistical data. It enables the readers to comprehend and interpret data quickly and to understand significant aspects at a glance. The work 'TABLE' is followed by the serial Roman number which is placed at the centre two spaces above the title of the table. The title of the table is written in capital letters at the centre of the page. The statistical data are presented in vertical columns and horizontal row, according to some classification of subject matter.

(e) Figures

A figure is a device that presents statistical data in pictorial or visual form. The figure is used to a variety of graphs, charts, maps, sketches, diagrams and drawings. It helps to understand the aspects of data clearly and easily. One idea or fact should be presented in each figure. The description of the figure must be given in the textual body. 'FIGURE' should be written in the centre of the page at the top of the figure. The title of the figure should be written in capital letters two spaces below the figure. The scale of the figure must be given.

(f) Pagination

Assigning page numbers of the report is very essential. The title page or initial page of any section does not have a page number typed on it, but a number is allotted to it in the series of pages. Page numbers are typed in the upper right hand corner, one inch below the top edge of the page.

The small or lower Roman numerals (i, ii, iii, iv,) are assigned for the pages of preliminary section. The serial Arabic nos. 1, 2, 3, 4.....so on are assigned for the pages of textual body or main body of the report i.e. Chapter I to last and Bibliography. The lower Roman numerals are assigned for the pages of appendices and index. The correct pagination depends upon the final edited copy or typed copy.

(g) Proof Reading

A research report should not have errors. It requires that final typed copies must be checked carefully. All types of errors should be deleted before submission. Thus, proof reading of final typed copies should be done two or three times.

(h) Binding and Submission

It is the last activity for preparing research report. Before giving to the binder it should be arranged properly and systematically and the serial number of pages are checked carefully. It should be given to an expert binder who has the experience of binding research thesis. Some universities require three copies of the thesis five copies of the abstract or summary and three copies of synopsis. These should also be prepared. A great precaution must be taken in printing the topic or title of the thesis that it must be the photo-state form of the topic which was approved by research degree committee. The covering page must be the same as inner cover given in preliminary section.

After binding the thesis it should be submitted to the university for evaluation purpose. Researcher should ascertain the date of submission and other requirement e.g. certificate of the supervisor. Evaluation fees etc. For the post-graduate dissertation. student should plan that he would be able to submit to college or university in time. He must obtain the receipt of the submission of his thesis.

Evaluation of a Research Report

The following questions are suggested relating to the various aspects of research report as a possible structure for the analysis:

1. The Title
   (*a*) Is it clear and concise?
   (*b*) Does it promise no more than the study can provide?

2. The Problem
   (*a*) Is it clearly stated?
   (*b*) Is it properly delimited?
   (*c*) Is its significance recognized?
   (*d*) Are specific questions raised and hypotheses are clearly stated?
   (*e*) Are the assumptions and limitations stated?
   (*f*) Are important terms defined?

3. Review of Related Literature
   (*a*) Is it adequately covered?
   (*b*) Are important findings-noted?
   (*c*) Is it well organized?
   (*d*) Is an effective summary provided?
   (*e*) Is the researcher commented adequately? Has he justified that his study is related to the studies and has the deviations from earlier studies.

4. Methodology Used for Conducting the Study
   (*a*) Is the research design described in detail?
   (*b*) Is the method adequate?
   (*c*) Is the population defined properly?
   (*d*) Is the sample described?
   (*c*) Are the relevant variables recognized?
   (*f*) Are appropriate controls provided?

(g) Are data collecting tools appropriate?

(h) Are validity and reliability established?

(i) Is the statistical treatment appropriate?

5. Data Analysis

(a) Is appropriate use made of tables and figures?

(b) Is the textual discussion clear and concise?

(c) Is the analysis of data relationships logical and perceptive?

(d) Is the statistical analysis accurately interpreted?

6. Conclusions and Suggestions

(a) Are the results discussed at length adequately?

(b) Are the inferences stated appropriately?

(c) Are the limitations of the findings enumerated clearly

(d) Are the applications of the findings suggested adequately?

(e) Are some suggestions for further studies proposed appropriately?

Apart from these aspects of research report, its literary presentation should be worth for publications. There should be minimum or no typing errors. The researcher should have the confidence aware of the limitations of his study.

Writing Research Papers

Research is a critical, disciplined, inquiry into a problem. A research paper is a presentation of the result of such a critical inquiry. Writing a research paper involves certain procedures which, is followed in proper sequence, might avoid waste of time, energy and resources. The writer of a research article has to rely on two kinds of source of information called as primary and secondary on the basis of the evaluation of their trust worthiness. Similarly, he has to be extremely cautious in the discrimination between facts and opinions though both are important elements in his arguments and chain of reasoning. A 'fact' is anything which is known to exist or which is accepted as true. There is no need to substantiate well known facts like the birth dates of contemporary leaders or events. A research paper has to present a number of opinions as expressed by others or researcher himself. It is necessary to document those opinions of others by pin-pointing their sources so that anyone if in doubt can verify any of them. It is a sound policy and good convention to keep facts separated from opinions, especially the author's own, in a research paper. Any mixture of them there will lower the credibility of the paper as a scholarly piece of writing.

Format of a Research Paper

There is no fixed format for writing a research paper. Each individual has to develop his own approach. But a broad guideline can be evolved on the basis of experiences of many researchers. An outline of the research paper should be prepared before details are written down. A good outline will help in the proper structuring or designing of a research paper. It will involve all the relevant points in an effective sequence which will provide direction to the flow of writing research paper. Before an outline is prepared, it will be necessary to make a list of all the points and to determine their status either as major, or supplementary materials. A working outline can be prepared by combining these points in a paper sequence.

The format of research paper usually includes three main points:

- An introduction,
- The main body of text and
- Conclusions.

It is possible to make a good beginning with a relevant quotation which is not too familiar. It should attract attention and arouse curiosity. A paper may begin by a good summary of the research paper or research work done on the topic in the past. It should be objective survey in very brief. The important references to the sources used for this survey will enable the writer to demonstrate familiarity with the key concepts, theories, latest developments in research and prevailing controversies.

The introduction is also a place where the central problem is clearly stated. The central theme should be brought into focus along with its significance. The main body of the paper should be developed to the report of the research work to the presentation of arguments based on the work of exploration, discoveries experiments, analysis, synthesis or all those activities which constituted the research and led to the conclusions. A research paper will have constructive and critical sides. The constructive paper should follow in order to prove how the research reported in the paper fills the void.

But another approach is equally welcome in which the contribution of the research is presented first. Its significance is highlighted by critical refutation of the claims of the rival theories. In any case, what the researcher has done should be brought into focus. The views of the researcher should be supported by references statistics and other form of evidences.

The paper should have a conclusion in which the quintessence of the work is reiterated preceded by a recapitulation of the main arguments or statements of the research work. The first draft of a paper may not be the most satisfactory though it may look so at the time of writing. Most experienced writers set aside the first draft for a few days, at least for a few hours. This process helps in a more impersonal critical and objective reappraisal. Any paper improves with revision or rewriting and the research paper is no exception. It will help the writer if he imagines himself addressing the most renowned scholars in the field while writing the paper in the first place and later in its finalization.

References

Creswell, J.W. (2005). Educational research: Planning, conducting and evaluating quantitative and qualitative research (2nd Ed), Upper saddle river, NJ: Pearson.

Cronbach LJ (1970). Essentials of Psychological Testing. Harper & Row.

Kemper.E., Stringfield. S., & Teddlie, C. (2005), "Mixed methods sampling strategies in social generic research," in A. Tashakkori & C. Teddlie (Eds), Handbook of mixed methods in social and behavioural research (pp 273–296) Thousand oaks, CA; Sage.

Kothari. C.R., "Research Methodology: Methods and Techniques," Second edition, New age International (P) Limited Publishers, New Delhi, 2004.

Naresh. K. Malhotra, David F. Birks (2007). Marketing Research: An Applied Approach, Prentice Hall, Inc., a Pearson Education company.

Pallant, Julie F. (Julie Florence) (2006). SPSS survival manual: a step by step guide to data analysis using SPSS.version 12, Allen unwin.

Singh, Y.K (2006). Fundamentals of Research Methodology and statistics. New age International Publishers.

(Author is deeply indebted to the above references and many other who may not be acknowledged here)

Printed in Great Britain
by Amazon